T0113676

COVID, Cancer, and Calling

A Memoir of Faith and Healing

QUENTIN W. GOODWIN

authorHOUSE®

AuthorHouse™
1663 Liberty Drive
Bloomington, IN 47403
www.authorhouse.com
Phone: 833-262-8899

Published by AuthorHouse 08/31/2022

ISBN: 978-1-6655-6963-7 (sc)
ISBN: 978-1-6655-6962-0 (e)

Print information available on the last page.

This book is printed on acid-free paper.

This book is dedicated to my wife, Renee Goodwin, and my children, Rylee and Rowan. Also, to my mother, Eartha Goodwin. Thank you for being my rock and inspiration throughout this period. I love you and will work tirelessly to become the husband, father, and son you deserve.

Additionally, I dedicate this book to the doctors, nurses, and staff at Atrium Health, Charlotte, North Carolina. Thank you for providing first-class service to patients and families. To all other doctors, nurses, researchers, ministers and clergy, teachers, bus drivers, grocery store and restaurant workers, truck drivers, and all other essential workers during the pandemic. Thank you for keeping us as safe as possible.

CONTENTS

INTRODUCTION

On Saturday, February 22, 2020, I witnessed one of the greatest basketball games in my life. Cannon School battled Charlotte Latin for the North Carolina 4A Independent Schools state championship. This game featured some outstanding players who have an excellent future in Division 1 college basketball, maybe even the NBA. More importantly for me, this game featured my godson Deuce, a Bahamas native who has been staying with us for three years while attending Cannon. Though he did not get a lot of playing time that game, my family and I were proud of the tremendous growth and development he realized throughout his investment in the program. For this reason, my entire family—Renee (my wife), Rylee and Rowan (our kids), and MeeMaw(my mother-in-law)—made it a priority that day to attend and support Cannon in this historic quest.

What an intense and electric atmosphere. The twenty-five-hundred-seat gymnasium was visibly at over-capacity, with enthusiastic students from both schools cheering on their respective teams, passionate parents and family members supporting their child, college scouts looking for their school's next basketball star, and basketball junkies fending for a great game. Whatever reason for attendance, this game delivered. Both teams fought hard, with each side making timely plays to keep their team in the game. In the end, Cannon School pulled off the win, 71–69, on a game-saving block of a three-pointer.

Looking back, this game was a significant event for my

family. For one, we were we able to support Deuce as he won the state championship. Even more significantly, this was the last family event we attended with a capacity crowd. This was the last event the family attended without wearing a mask, without socially distancing, and without frequently applying hand sanitizer. You see, as this game was taking place, COVID-19 was steadily spreading throughout the United States, and little did we know that in just a few weeks, our lives would change drastically.

I am extremely gratefully that my family followed the various protocol measures and thus far have been spared from contracting the virus. We all were able to work and attend school in proactively safe environments. The kids endured challenging classroom environments, both virtually and in-person, to successfully complete their kindergarten and second school years. Renee's enrichment center business expanded into its second location, realizing tremendous growth in its fifth year of operation. Deuce and Cannon won its second state basketball championship, and he contributed tremendously with leadership, hustle, and timely plays. He also earned a track and field scholarship after breaking various school records. MeeMaw is closing on a new home a few miles from us, which is a great achievement amid this challenging housing market. So overall, my family realized many blessings, for which we are extremely grateful.

Personally, this period presented great opportunities for spiritual growth and development as I continue my calling into ministry in the United Methodist Church. I was able to adapt and perform successfully in my at-home work environment; though I missed being in the office, I was able to connect with my teammates to ensure our work is performed in an efficient manner. Additionally, and personally most importantly, working from home allowed me to spend more time with my kids before and after school—seeing them off as they board the school bus, and welcoming them back home in the afternoon.

As the world continues to transition into one under the radar of COVID-19, I became more and more thankful for God keeping my family physically safe and financially stable from the virus. We endured numerous challenges and learned great faith lessons during the eighteen-month period. In June 2021, these faith lessons were quickly put to the test.

Starting in late 2020, I began experiencing nagging pain in my hips and lower back. Since it occurred after I worked out on the treadmill or spin bike, I attributed that pain to hip pointers due to inadequate stretching. Though I was still able to walk, work out, and do yard work, I felt the pain getting gradually worse. In early May, I finally listened to Renee's advice and made an appointment with my family doctor, who then referred me to a sports medicine specialist. An x-ray found a hairline fracture in my right hip, along with muscle tears; subsequently, the doctor set up a series of physical therapy sessions along with pain medicine.

Physical therapy worked for a while. In time, I went from walking on two crutches, to walking on one crutch, to moving without crutches. I still could not bend, climb stairs, or move laterally, but I felt confident that I was on the right road to recovery. Six weeks into the treatment, however, the pain suddenly came back with a vengeance. It got to the point where I had to go to the emergency room—which in hindsight proved to be a waste of time, in that they just gave me a shot in the arm and prescribed more steroids.

Finally, the Monday after Father's Day, I decided to push for an MRI with my insurance company and doctors, for this would dig deeper into what was causing this excruciating pain. I called 911, and they transported me to the Atrium Emergency Room in Lincolnton, North Carolina. Though

Lincolnton was not the closest Atrium facility, we immediately felt satisfied with the decision to be taken there. Upon check-in, the nurses and doctors took great care in asking questions and learning about my troubles, and from their initially research, they immediately resolved to get the MRI. Well, the MRI found a mass in the sacrum bone of my pelvic area. The sacrum contains nerves that protrude down the hips into the thighs and hamstrings.

Based on the MRI results, they ordered a biopsy to determine the severity of the mass. Subsequently, I was transferred to the Atrium Levine Cancer Center in Charlotte, where I received great care from the entire staff. After the biopsy and additional blood tests, I was diagnosed with multiple myeloma. Multiple myeloma is a cancer that affects the white blood cells and damages bone tissues in various areas. The cancer negatively affects the body's capacity to fight off infections by crowding out the healthy plasma cells, thus weakening the immune system. In my case, the myeloma pretty much targeted my sacrum bone, causing lesions similar to termites eating away wood. The encouraging news was that, though not curable, this cancer is highly treatable, where one can live a productive life while in remission. Additionally, there is a tremendous amount of research currently being performed to find innovative ways to treat, and possibly cure, multiple myeloma.

I am writing this paragraph six weeks into my chemotherapy treatment. Additionally, I completed a two-week radiation session designed to reduce the pain and shrink the cancer cells within the sacrum and T-7 areas. Though the pain still persists, and knowing that I have a long way to go in this recovery process, I find myself moving around tremendously better, particularly walking with a more natural gait and gradually bending and squatting better. I am truly thankful the treatment has allowed my family to see me move around pain-free and gradually getting better.

> Consider it pure joy, my brothers and sisters, whenever you face trials of many kinds, because you know that the testing of your faith produces perseverance. Let perseverance finish its work so that you may be mature and complete, not lacking anything. (James 1:2–4)

I was born and raised in South Carolina and am a life-long member of the United Methodist Church. My father served as an elder in the South Carolina Conference for over fifty years, most notably serving sixteen years as pastor of a five-church parish in the Sea Islands (Johns, Wadmalaw, Younges, James, and Edisto Islands). My mother served in the South Carolina Public School System for over forty years and was one of the first African American speech pathologists in the state. Even with her hectic schedule, my mom diligently supported my dad by actively participating in church activities such as the Senior Choir, United Methodist Women, and Stewardess Board. They also kept my two brothers and me actively involved in the children and youth activities. A typical Sunday in my early years consisted of 1) riding an hour with my mom to my dad's first church service, which starts at 9:00 a.m., 2) leaving that service immediately after my dad finishes his sermon, 3) eating lunch that my mom prepared for us in the car while travelling to the second service, 4) struggling to stay awake during the second service, and 5) returning home, hopefully in time for the second half of the NFL game.

Growing up as a preacher's kid presented numerous challenges and expectations. I consistently felt that everyone expected me to follow in my dad's footsteps into the ministry. I sense that this expectation initially drove me away from considering the ministry. In my mind, there was room for only one "Rev. Goodwin" in the family.

After graduating from the College of Charleston in 1992, I moved to Charlotte to begin my professional career. I did not find a church home in Charlotte until late 1993, when I stumbled across Simpson-Gillespie United Methodist Church. After joining the church, I was afforded numerous ministry and leadership positions. Also, I began to receive encouragement from numerous members to explore the ministry—to quote one of my mentors: "Quentin, you are missing your calling." Needless to say, others were seeing God's calling in my life, the calling from which I had been running.

For years, I have been running from God's call, coming up with every excuse possible to not pursue the ministry. "I have no money for seminary." "I have no time for seminary." "I am satisfied with the job I have now." "I can never be the preacher that my dad was." Through it all, thankfully, God patiently worked through the excuses and kept His call in my system. In 2019, I finally answered the call and began the journey to ministry, and in May 2020, the Metro District's Committee on Ordained Ministry certified me as a candidate for local pastor.

COVID. Cancer. Calling. Three life changing events in three years. Three events connected by the life lessons learned from each instance.

Throughout my spiritual life, I have been taught that God places challenges in your life to prepare you for greater blessings He has in store for you. Regardless of the pain you suffer through the challenge, it is meant to teach you valuable lessons to make you a stronger person. Moreover, your test becomes your testimony, your setback becomes your setup for blessings, your trial becomes your triumph, your mess becomes your message, and your vulnerability becomes your victory. My faith in knowing that I am God's child, created with a plan and purpose, gives me the confidence to fulfill that purpose and do His will. From the calling to COVID to cancer, 2019–2021 provided tremendous valuable lessons that have prepared me for the service God is calling me to do, and I look forward to fulfilling His call.

Trust God's Plan

"For I know the plans I have for you," declares the Lord, "plans to prosper you and not to harm you, plans to give you hope and a future. Then you will call on me and come and pray to me, and I will listen to you. You will seek me and find me when you seek me with all your heart. I will be found by you," declares the Lord, "and will bring you back from captivity." (Jeremiah 29:11–14)

I can say that, throughout my life, I have been a resourceful person. I believe I inherited this trait from my maternal grandparents, Harry and Mamie Lee Dowling, who I observed using natural resources and talents to make homemade fig and pear preserve, natural sugar, lye soap, and quilts. I haven't gotten to the point of butchering hogs or cleaning chickens, but I am perfecting the craft of making sausage and liver pudding. Regardless of whether my product turns out right or not, I appreciate the thrill of trying to make things on my own rather than simply buying them.

During the lockdown, I found myself embarking on numerous projects around the house. Some of these projects were needed repairs, some were to satisfy my wife's wish list, and some were COVID projects to keep my mind active during the pandemic shutdown. My first projects entailed improving our back yard, where I set paved stones to expand our patio, put together a pergola that Renee bought from Sam's Club, and made a pretty neat (I must proudly say) outdoor table to assist in our barbecue prep. From my stay-at-home time watching *Man, Fire, Food* on the Cooking Channel, I constructed a smoker from a wine barrel and a portable outdoor oven that can cook a whole animal. Inside the house, I was able (to my wife's surprise) to install a ceiling fan in our playroom. Ironically, my last project was in November 2020, when I made a Charleston-style joggling bench for my uncle, Dave Hooks, who was just diagnosed with Lymphoma. I made it as a sign of support for him as he embarked on his journey to recovery.

With each project, I relied on a detailed plan by the manufacturer. Each plan presented the materials, including cutting size of the boards, step-by-step instructions for installing the product, and spare parts in case the sizes did not fit properly. Needless to say, I felt much more confident in my project when I had such a plan to guide me through the process. Even when tempted to deviate from the plan, I was glad to have that plan in hand to get me back on track in realizing the completion goal.

COVID

As with my projects, our COVID ordeal taught me to rely heavily on God's plan, and leaning on that plan makes it much easier to navigate through the many challenges the pandemic presents. As a believer, I know that God created me with a definite purpose in life, and through prayer, scripture, and obeying His Word, I will get that much closer to realizing His plan and vision. Even through seemingly impossible challenges like COVID, God provides the necessary resources to get us through and back on track to continue our fulfillment of His plan.

For churches and worship communities, God provided the valuable resource of technology to allow them to continue His work during the shutdown. It was great to see the many worship services, particularly those churches I grew up in, streaming live on Facebook, Zoom, and YouTube on Sunday mornings. This allowed me to connect with and support them in a virtual environment. My church, Simpson-Gillespie United Methodist Church, was blessed to have been appointed a pastor with experience in videography and streaming production. Upon the announcement of the COVID shutdown of physical church worship and meetings, Rev. Dayson immediately set up our virtual streaming platforms to continue spreading God's Word without missing a beat. And for a church with predominately older members typically lukewarm to technology (and probably the only church in Charlotte that still uses a cassette tape player), we quickly realized tremendous benefits from this new experience. Not only did we reach out to former members who moved away and homebound members, we saw regular attendance from international worshippers.

Financially, we were able to maintain our stewardship level through the online and text giving portal we set up a few years earlier. Additionally, our outreach ministry provided much-needed services to our community through drive-through pizza and prayer parties, our community blessing box, and offering our site for COVID testing. Things went so well for us, our church council approved the investment of additional technological equipment to continue our online ministry post-pandemic.

God provided the technology to continue His plan for Simpson-Gillespie United Methodist Church.

Though many small businesses suffered drastically during the shutdown, many corporations were able to operate successfully in an online environment. Even with their employees converting to a work-from-home environment, these companies experienced little to no drop-off in operations and services. Prior to the shutdown, my employer invested in the technology necessary for each employee to work from home in case of a disaster or act of nature. Their investment allowed us to more easily transition to a 100 percent work-from-home schedule for an extended period. We were able to maintain, and in some periods exceed, our production and quality requirements; through virtual enrichment events and company-wide meetings and updates, we enhanced our virtual capabilities to allow employees to remain connected with each other.

God provided the technology to continue His plan for my employer, the London Stock Exchange Group (LSEG).

Our schools faced major challenges as they tried their best to continue school in a safe and responsible manner. Many of our larger school districts, colleges, and universities across the country were compelled to follow a strictly online format because they simply could not provide a safe environment for students and teachers. They quickly realized the difficulties that the technological divide historically posed for many students. This exposure compelled our political leaders to work diligently toward incorporating enhanced and affordable technology into its nationwide infrastructure plan. Those who did have the capabilities to continue online learning found it really difficult to adapt successfully to this new environment. Teachers found themselves working more hours than usual trying to maintain their class responsibilities—for little or no extra money. Parents found themselves juggling their time between remote working and managing their child's online class responsibilities.

Our children's' schools fared slightly better. In March 2020, Rylee and Rowan transitioned to an online environment and then finished their school year. It was truly fun to see them learn, navigate, and interact with their fellow classmates via Zoom. They began the 2020–21 year with the option of attending school physically or continuing with remote learning. After studying the school's COVID protocols and procedures, Renee and I felt confident enough to have them go back to school physically. The school required everyone to wear masks indoors, reconstructed classrooms and hallways to provide adequate spacing between students, and required parents to complete electronic daily screenings before their child could be allowed to attend school. There were still some difficulties that arose during the school year, with various breakouts among students and teachers. We had to start the first month after winter break back to the online format. Still, our children finished the school year strong academically.

Deuce's school converted to online learning the same day as Rylee and Rowan, and he started the 2020–21 year with a hybrid learning environment. To ensure proper spacing, the school separated its students alphabetically and adopted a "two-week on-campus, one-week remote" schedule for them. Parents had to complete electronic daily screenings before their child was allowed to attend school on campus. Additionally, Renee and I faced the challenge of managing Deuce's final year athletically. He attended a private school that operated under the North Carolina Independent Athletic Association. Unlike public schools, they were allowed to continue their athletic schedule, under strict guidelines. Other than parents, there were no fans in attendance at games, and each parent had to wear a mask and undergo temperature checks before being admitted into games. Each school had to undergo enhanced cleaning of its facility before each game. Most interestingly, each player had to wear a mask during the game. We were confident in the plan his school put together to maintain a safe environment for its students and were happy that Deuce was able to complete his senior year in as close to normal manner as possible. Not only was he able to finish his basketball career with second consecutive state championship, but he was also able to participate in a full season of track and field, during which he set school records in the 100- and 200-meter events.

Despite these challenges, God provided the technology, and will provide the educational resources, to continue His plan for His children at Mountain Island Charter and Cannon Schools.

After the onset of the virus, our government officials worked diligently to provide the resources to get us back to a safe and normal environment. They invested in pharmaceutical companies to quickly develop vaccines for its citizens to control the spread of COVID. The Centers for Disease Control and Prevention provided constant updates to educate everyone on how to protect themselves from contracting the disease. Unfortunately, these government measures were mired in controversy, as a symptom of our toxic political environment. Generally, Democrats promoted the idea of "Trust the Science," quickly adhering to the suggestions of masking up, social distancing, and taking the vaccine, whereas Republicans were more hesitant and quickly endorsed the "Don't Tread on Me" and "Protect Our Freedoms" philosophy and adopted more lax measures to promote herd immunity.

Despite the confusion and misinformation, God provided the medical resources to protect His people and fulfill the promise He made to Abraham.

Cancer

As I reflect on my cancer journey, I appreciate the plan God provided to me. This appreciation makes it that much easier to accept the fact that He presented these challenges to prepare me for greater things.

After hearing from the oncologists, I sent a text to my physical therapist, who began working with me and suggested that my problems were more severe than the initial diagnosis from my family doctor. He immediately responded with this message: "Accurate diagnosis is the first step to effective treatment." This text provided some assurance that I was in the right place and had the best care team to put together an effective treatment plan to put the cancer in remission and keep it there. I knew right then that I had to trust the doctors' plan.

Before my hospital admission, I spent most of my time on the internet researching possible causes of my pain. I even wasted money on various products that promised to relieve and cure my pain. As soon as I received the diagnosis and treatment plan, my self-research immediately ceased. I received an accurate diagnosis, and now it was time to trust the effective treatment. God provided an award-winning team of experienced doctors focused on treating multiple myeloma, a team with far more experience than someone researching the internet. It was time to trust the plan.

This was not an easy task for me. Despite the assurances that my bloodwork showed great progression, I found myself easily frustrated with the continuous pain in my affected area. For the first time in my life, I had to be wheeled into the doctor's office for my initial appointments and treatments; this hurt my pride tremendously. I became increasingly weary from my body being frequently poked to draw blood and infuse the chemo treatment. I had to rely on others to do simple tasks such as washing, using the bathroom, cutting my hair, and taking long walks. I was not able to sleep upstairs in my bed for about three months; being separated from my wife in this manner took a tremendous toll on my manhood. I was not able to do my dad duties with Rylee and Rowan, though I came to appreciate logging in and playing Roblox with them. Though I appreciated the support, I became frustrated hearing stories from others about friends and family members who were diagnosed with multiple myeloma and were now thriving with normal life. Hearing this, my thoughts were, *Yes, good for them, but this is my life. What if this doesn't work for me? It sure doesn't feel like it now.*

Still, with all the negative thoughts, with all the pain, with all the frustration, I had to think long term and trust the process.

Calling

In December 2019, after years of running and making excuses, I made the decision to answer God's call to ministry in the United Methodist Church. Upon intensive consultation with my pastor—and constant prayer, devotion, and reflection—I decided to begin the journey to become a local pastor within the church. The first part of the journey was to participate in a conference-wide mentorship group, where we met monthly to intensively explore and discern our calling. Not only did these sessions prepare us for our initial interview with the District Committee on Ministry, they also allowed us to explore our personal strengths and weaknesses in preparation for ministry. During my discernment process, I realized that a major growth opportunity is providing clinical care to members. Whether it be through visitation, phone calls, or love gifts, I found myself continuously falling short in this area. God started working on improving this weakness by presenting the opportunity to serve as a class leader in my church. With this role, I was assigned a group of around ten members to follow up with on a frequent basis and report to my pastor any needs that required his attention. I found this experience rewarding in that I became more comfortable with serving my fellow members through visitation and membership care.

God made me realize the importance of membership care during my time in the hospital waiting for my diagnosis. I was deeply affected by the level of support from my family and friends. Their acts of love, compassion, and prayer greatly eased the anxiety and uncertainty Renee and I felt as we awaited the medical team's action plan. While I appreciated the support, my mind continued to be led to those who were alone during their times of waiting and anxiety. Before this time, I never thought how much of a mental toll cancer takes on someone; nonetheless, a strong support system is needed during this time. My cancer experience compelled me to reconsider my ministry track within the United Methodist Church. While I knew I would enjoy leading a local congregation, I feel a greater opportunity ministering through chaplaincy, particularly to those dealing with health issues such as cancer. Whichever track God leads me to, I know and trust that He has prepared me to become a stronger pastoral care provider for the people I am appointed to serve.

I became more confident in His plan after I had two memorable conversations with friends who shared their life-changing experiences after they answered God's call.

The first conversation was with the manager of a Caribbean-style bed-and-breakfast property in Charlotte. For my birthday in August 2021, Renee and I spent a getaway weekend at her beautiful property within the affluent Cotswald neighborhood. We were blessed to have Uncle Dave (who recently finished his chemotherapy and won his battle with lung cancer) and Aunt Angy come up from Moncks Corner and spend the weekend with us there. Though we enjoyed the awesome food, warm hospitality, and peacefully accommodations, I found our conversations with the manager the most memorable part of the weekend.

She shared that she answered God's call to purchase the property in Cotswald and convert it to a bed-and-breakfast in honor of her mother and grandmother. Her first years in business presented major challenges with her neighbors, who frequently challenged her zoning capabilities. At one point, the neighbors successfully appealed her zoning license, thus forcing her to close the business. After this crushing defeat, she decided to visit her family in Trinidad for further reflection and discernment. She shared that. One morning during her visit, God led her to walk on the beach. She was at her lowest point and did not know where to turn, but while on the beach, God led her to a bench close to the water. There God spoke to her and asked her if she remembered why He initially called her to open a bed-and-breakfast. He reminded her that His plan was to provide a place of spiritual reflection and renewal for His people. Somehow, she forgot that purpose and was deviating from His plan by doing things her way. God used that defeat to get her back on track in fulfilling and trusting His plan. Rejuvenated, she returned to Charlotte and eventually won her case, which allowed her to reopen her business, in accordance with God's plan. Today, she is realizing great success in providing spiritual resources to her visitors.

The second conversation was with my childhood friend and close fraternity brother, Terrance Moore. Terrance is now serving as pastor of a church in Milwaukee, Wisconsin, along with his wife. During our conversation, he shared that at the onset of his call discernment, he was diagnosed with Hodgkin's disease. During his successful treatment, he found himself in deep conversation with God. From those conversations, he found that God used his cancer experience to impel him to reflect on whether he was going into ministry for the right reasons. Should he continue to do things his way, or was he ready to trust God's plan completely and without fail?

His story continued; at one point during the process, the doctors gave him the option to continue the treatment, since they saw the cancer being undetectable much earlier than projected. After prayer and reflection, he decided to continue and finish the treatment because it allowed him to further connect with God and completely trust His plan. He shared that his cancer experience led him to become a much stronger and confident servant for God's people.

I am thankful that these friends shared their respective stories of triumph over tragedy; their stories empowered me to become more confident that I will come out of my cancer challenge with the same result: a much stronger and confident servant of God, trusting in the plan He has for my life.

God's Plan Never Fails

> Many are the plans in the minds of man, but
> it is the purpose of the Lord that will stand.
> (Psalm 19:21)

I received memorable advice from a pastor during the ordination ceremony for my cousin, who was confirmed as an elder in the African American Episcopal church. He observed,

"Once God calls you, he never forgets you." As I reflect on this thought, I am reminded of God's promise to Abraham in Genesis 17. He promised that "if you obey me and always do right, I will keep my promise to you and give you more descendants than can be counted. I will give you and them the land in which you are now a foreigner."

The Bible is filled with stories that shows God fulfilling this promise. Through flood and famine, through slavery and deception, through despair, doubt, and disobedience, God took care of His people and fulfilled His plan. As He did then, He will do the same for us. All we have to do is trust and obey Him completely. We cannot infuse our plans into His, no matter how much we know (or think we know). Rather, trust Him completely, and He will take care of you.

Part of my treatment plan was to take a series of medicine on a daily basis. I was prescribed two sets of pain medicine, one medicine to manage my immune system, two sets of medicine to control my digestive system, and two sets of medicine to control constipation. Upon receiving this plan from the palliative care team, I expressed my concern with taking so much medicine, particularly the pain medicine. I always had reservations about taking pain medicine on a regular basis because of my fear that it would lead to uncontrolled dependency. Additionally, I expressed concern that these medicines could affect brain cells and cause mental damage in the long run. Additionally, from watching the commercials, it seems as though the side effects of the medicine outweigh the benefits of its original treatment. Though the team appreciated my concern for these matters, they assured me that these medicines were a vital part of the plan to recovery, and they would continually monitor my well-being throughout the process. I just needed to communicate with them if I realized any mood shift, dependency, or physical changes.

From this consultation, I resolved to diminish my own thoughts and rely on the more experienced team to care for me with their plan. This team has a record of success with patients who went into long-term remission from the plan. The plan did not fail for them, so it should not fail for me. For this reason, I felt more comfortable with proceeding with the process.

I share this story with thoughts of those struggling with the choice of taking the vaccine for the Corona virus. While I don't empathize with those who refuse to take the vaccine for political purposes, I do understand those who do not want to take it because of concerns about how the medicine affects their body. The same reservations I have about my treatment medicine, they have concerns about the virus vaccine. Here's my advice to those struggling with this: trust and believe that God has provided gifted hands to develop these vaccines to take care of His people. These vaccines have a 95 percent efficacy rate against serious illness from COVID, so out of the one or two instances we hear about the death of a vaccinated person from COVID, there are millions more who have successfully taken the vaccine and are much more protected from the virus. If you do get infected somehow, there is a much greater chance of you not coming down with serious illness. This process is part of God's plan to care for His people through this crisis, so put your trust in Him rather than your own reservations.

God will never leave or fail us. Through Him, we will always receive the victory He promises for us. All we have to do is put all our trust in Him, obey His Word, and lean not on our own understanding.

God's Plan Never Wavers

> Heaven and earth will pass away, but My words will by no means pass away. (Matthew 24:35)

We live in an environment under constant change. The internet changed the way we research, shop, and communicate. 9/11 changed the way we travel. COVID changed the way we congregate. Relationships change, attitudes change, methods change. It seems that we continuously have to adapt to constant changes. However, it is comforting to know that God never changes. As He was yesterday, He is the God today and will be the same God tomorrow. He does not have to adapt to any changes in our environment, simply because of His omnipotent power. You must put your trust in His perfection, because He will never fail in His perfect plan for you.

I refer back to the conversations I had with my two friends about how, despite their wanting to do God's plan their own way, God presented challenges to remind them to trust completely in His process, for His path to victory and success will always prevail, according to His will. Though we may not understand at the time, we must constantly put our hands in His unchanging hands and trust in the plan He has for us. God loves you and will never let you down; you will receive the victory in the long run. Daryl Coley ministers to us through his lyrics: "He's preparing me for something I cannot handle now. He's making me ready just because he cares. He's providing me with what I'll need to carry out the next matter in my life."

God created you with a special purpose and plan to fulfill. This plan never changes and will always be fulfilled if we trust Him completely and follow His Word. Because He loves us, He will place challenges in our lives to bring us back to fulfilling His plan. We must know that these challenges are His way to bring us back to His call. Because He called us, He will never forget us.

Throughout the pain, throughout the doubt, throughout the despair, I appreciate God using this illness to work on the weaknesses I realized as I discerned my calling. He put this challenge in my life to prepare for the continued fulfillment of His plan and purpose for my life. His plan never changed and will never change as I continue to trust in Him and trust the process.

God's Plan Is Mysterious

> For my thoughts are not your thoughts, neither are your ways my ways, declares the LORD. For as the heavens are higher than the earth, so are my ways higher than your ways and my thoughts than your thoughts. (Isaiah 55:8–9)

As we continue through our faith journey, we find it an amazing experience as God reveals Himself to us in such mysterious and powerful ways. From these experiences, we gain greater knowledge of our omnipotent, omnipresent, and omniscient God. Yet there may be those frustrating times where we deal with difficult situations, where we cannot find the right answers to what we desire to understand. We don't know a lot, but we do know that we worship a God Who loved us so much that He sacrificed His Son for our sake. And by simply trusting and believing, God will grant us all we need to endure this world and secure an everlasting life of peace beyond this place.

Truly, God works in mysterious ways to reveal His plan in our lives. We do not know when, how, or why He allows things to happen to us; still, we should know and have the faith that our present situation is not the end but only a vital step towards our final victory, which is life eternal.

Stay close to God, and He will always be with you, and boy, do we need that assurance as we deal in this world.

This world will still bring you uncertainty and disappointment, but know that in the end, all things work together for good for those who are called according to His purpose.

This world will still bring injustice, unfairness, and division, but know that in the end, God will judge the righteous and the wicked, for there is a time for every matter, for every work.

This world will still bring you tests and trials, but know that in the end, blessed is the man who remains steadfast under trial, for he will receive the crown of life, which God has promised to those who love Him.

This world will still bring defeat and death, but thanks be to God, Who in the end gives us the victory through our Lord Jesus Christ. Therefore, my beloved brothers, be steadfast, immovable, always abounding in the work of the Lord, knowing that in the Lord, your labor is not in vain.

Virtual Ministry

This page is dedicated to the many churches who adapted their respective ministries to provide virtual worship services, Bible studies, and other programs. Many of these churches went beyond their comfort zones to minister to others in this unique format, thus continuing to spread God's Word during the pandemic. Personally, I thank the following churches for ministering to me virtually at some point during this time:

Simpson-Gillespie United Methodist Church, Charlotte, NC
Wesley United Methodist Church, Johns Island, SC
Rev. Kairos International Christian Church, Milwaukee, WI
Bethlehem-St. James United Methodist
Church, Johns Island, SC
Hope Community Christian Church, Greensboro, NC
Northeast Baptist Church, Philadelphia, PA
Emmanuel United Methodist Church, Sumter, SC
St. Andrews United Methodist Church, Hilton Head, SC
Reid Chapel AME Church, Columbia, SC
Harmony United Methodist Church, Rock Hill, SC
Holy Trinity AME Church, Mount Pleasant, SC
Mt. Sinai AME Church, Elgin, SC
St. Mark United Methodist Church, Taylors, SC
St. Stephen United Methodist Church, Orangeburg, SC
Centenary United Methodist Church, Moncks Corner, SC
Believers Embassy International, Nassau, Bahamas
New Hope United Methodist Church, Rock Hill, SC
True Worship Christian Fellowship Church, Atlanta, GA
White Oak Missionary Baptist Church, Sumter, SC
St. Ambrose Anglican Church, Nassau, Bahamas

You Cannot Do It Alone

Abide in me, and I in you. As the branch cannot bear fruit of itself, except it abide in the vine; no more can ye, except ye abide in me. I am the vine, ye are the branches: He that abideth in me, and I in him, the same bringeth forth much fruit: for without me ye can do nothing. (John 15:4–5)

COVID

While we witnessed unprecedented death and despair from the COVID pandemic, we also observed instances where communities came together in love and support for each other. We saw continued support and appreciation for our doctors and nurses who were traumatized, not only by being overworked from the emergency rooms filled to over-capacity with COVID patients, but also by helplessly witnessing numerous patients die alone from the disease. We saw governments come together in bipartisan fashion to provide relief to businesses and families greatly affected by the economic impact from the COVID shutdown. We saw community groups come together to provide food and other resources to those in dire need during the pandemic. The world came together to pray for and support each other; with this came the much-needed comfort that we were not in this situation alone, and together we will get past this pandemic.

During this time, the world also observed two events where people came together to effect change.

On May 25, 2020, in Minneapolis, Minnesota, George Floyd was killed while being apprehended by the police. Video camera footage showed the knee of police officer Derek Chauvin pressed on the back of Floyd's neck for approximately nine minutes, while four fellow officers observed with seeming approval of this excessive use of force. Despite continuous desperate pleas from the crowd, the officer's knee remained on Floyd's neck until he lost consciousness and eventually passed away. This terrible event was followed by weeks of worldwide protests from millions of people crying out for social justice and police reform. Though other police-related deaths of black men were followed by similar protests, this incident proved to be different in that it woke the conscience of America and the world.

The world came together to say enough was enough, and something needed to be done to let African Americans know that their lives matter and they deserve equal access to the tremendous opportunities for success in this world.

Sports leagues used their platform to call for social justice—from various messages placed on uniforms and playing surfaces to the playing of "Lift Every Voice and Sing" before the National Anthem before games.

Most importantly, we saw accountability. Police officers and commissioners became increasingly subject to discipline, which included termination, in response to reports of abuse of power and mistreatment of black and disadvantaged people. Though we have a long way to go, it was good to see those in uniform finally being held accountable for their actions.

In May 2021, a jury found Chauvin guilty of second-degree murder. He was subsequently sentenced to twenty-two and a half years in prison. The remaining three officers were found guilty by a federal court of violating Floyd's civil rights. One of the officers pleaded guilty to aiding and abetting second-degree manslaughter in the criminal case; the remaining two officers await their trial as of this writing.

Though we await the Senate to finally pass the George Floyd Justice in Policing Act, which creates accountability measures for our police officers, we are thankful to have this important issue finally being brought to light, to the point that something needed to be done to change the way African Americans are treated by the police.

The world came together to effect change. We could not have done it alone.

Secondly, we observed the 2020 presidential election. Many viewed this election as the most important in our lifetime. Vice President Biden viewed this election as a battle for soul of our nation. Many in agreement came out in record form to express their voice and vote for change. Despite the challenges from the pandemic, despite the various voting laws which restricted voting for many individuals, and despite the intimidation tactics from numerous vigilante groups, Americans came out in droves to vote. President Trump received over 77 million votes, which was the second most received for any presidential candidate in an election. However, this was second only to his opponent, Joe Biden, who received a record 81 million votes and won in a landslide.

America came together to effect change. We could not have done it alone.

Cancer

One of my favorite stories in the Bible occurs in Exodus 17, where the Amalekites attacked Moses and the Israelites at Rephidim. After choosing his best men to battle the enemy, Moses went up to the hill with the staff of God in his hands. Whenever Moses raised his hands, the Israelites would win the battle, and whenever he lowered his hand, the Israelites began to lose. Verse 12 states that whenever Aaron and Hur saw Moses become weary, they would prop his arms up, Aaron on one side and Hur on the other, so his hand would remain steady until the Israelites secured the victory.

Where would Moses be without his partners?

Where would I be without my partners?

I am thankful for the many partners in my life who are propping me up in support throughout my bout with cancer. These partners provided an abundance of encouragement when I needed it most. I can truly say that it would have been much harder to survive without their timely support.

God

Emmanuel = God is with us.

I felt the worst pain in my life on Father's Day weekend. Nothing seemed to work to ease this pain; the steroids prescribed by the sports medicine doctor, the stretches suggested by the physical therapists, the guaranteed pain relief devices from my internet research purchased through Amazon. I was in a desperate state of mind, for I was never in this situation in my life. One Sunday morning, despite the pain, I decided to join my family in streaming Simpson Gillespie's worship service. Rev. Dayson's message was based on the story of Jesus walking on water during the storm to be with His disciples. From this story, he reiterated that God is with me during the storm and will provide whatever I need to get through it. I continually rely on this message throughout my treatment process, for it reminds me of the unparalleled partnership with God. He provided a tremendous hospital staff to care for me. He provided friends and family to support me throughout the treatment. He provided unconventional angels to minister to me in a timely manner. From this experience, I realize that effective partnership starts with a relationship with God. As I trust and believe in Him, He will provide all I need to get through any situation.

Renee

My wife has been a wonderful and reliable partner throughout this journey. From stepping up to take care of the children while I could not do my share of parental duties, to scheduling and transporting me to my appointments (especially the early morning radiation treatments), to arranging the lawn care and the housekeeping to ensure a safe and sanitary environment for me in the house, I can truly say that she has been a blessing to me and the family. Her partners at Mountain Island Charter School set up a meal tree to provide dinner to us every other day.

The most important aspect of our partnership through this process is her patience and understanding through my mood changes and frustrations. We only had one argument during this time, but from that incident, I learned to openly and frequently communicate my feelings to her—and listen to her and understand her feelings in return. I remember one day when I was really down, mentally and physically. When Renee came home from work and became aware of my situation, she felt like there was nothing she could do to make me feel better. She immediately began to pray. Her prayer gave me so much comfort and relief that day; the spirit that entered my heart empowered me to fight through the pain and continue to process with a positive attitude. Thank God for the power of intercessory prayer, especially from my loving wife.

Mom

As my father fell into unconsciousness in his hospital bed—about a week before his passing—he uttered to me, "Take care of your mother." These were the last words he said to me. I took his charge to heart and made it a priority going forward to protect and cherish his most precious legacy. I made sure to talk to Mom at least every other day and visit her as much as possible. Thankfully, my brother Irvin eventually moved back home due to a job transfer. During that time, Mom's mobility began to decline, to the point of her using a wheelchair. Irvin and his wife were able to transport Mom to her doctor's appointments and other important visits and accepted the role of Mom's primary caregivers.

Since my illness began in April, I have not been able to drive to Johns Island to visit Mom; this was probably the most disappointing part of this whole ordeal. However, I was still able to call her almost every day; not only to check on her, but to also update her on how I was feeling. Though there were times where she did not understand what I was going through, just hearing her voice provided great strength to make it through the rest of the day.

Irvin brought her up to visit three times during my illness. The first time was before the diagnosis, while I was going to physical therapy. There she saw my pain and agony as I tried to move around. The second visit was on my birthday. They decided to surprise me as I was going through the first round of chemotherapy. This visit, she saw an improvement in my mobility, as I was walking without any assistance. The last visit occurred the weekend before my stem cell transplant operation. Though she saw me walking normally and without any pain, she expressed concern over the whole procedure. I assured her that I would be okay and was in great hands with the medical team at Levine. We prayed and shared communion together, which really touched my spirit.

I appreciate my mom being Mom throughout my life, always being there to encourage and uplift me whenever I needed her. Whether it be to help pack my items and move, take care of the kids, or cheer us on during basketball games, plays, and dance recitals, Mom was always there. I will forever cherish the aforementioned visits where even though she was physically weak, she gave me great strength and encouraged me to push through the process. Truly, there is nothing like a mother's love, and there is nothing like a mother's partnership.

Tom

On Father's Day, Rylee gave me a toy dog with the caption "#1 Father" on his collar. We agreed to name the dog Tom. The next day, the lingering pain was so bad, I called 911 to be transported to the hospital. At the last minute, I decided to take Tom along with me for the ride. Tom became a reliable partner with me during the week-long hospital stay, for he was with me during every blood draw, MRI, and biopsy. He quickly became a favorite of the hospital staff after I shared the story of why he was here with me. Whenever Renee had to leave for the day, I would draw Tom closer to me as a reminder of the love and support from my family. He continues to be a reliable partner for the family, for he was with Rylee and Rowan to comfort them during their flu shots and COVID vaccinations. Truly, Tom made my hospital stay much more comfortable, and I remain thankful to have him as a partner.

Fraternity Brothers

I remain close to my fraternity brothers from college: Jon Bryant, a Secret Service agent in the DC area; Byron Gipson, a solicitor in Columbia, SC; Patrick Simmons, a retired Army officer in Columbia; and Bacchus Rolle, Deuce's father, who is the Minister of Public Utilities in Nassau, Bahamas. I believe the reason we bonded so well back then is that we cherished the one main trait we share: We are each our momma's baby boy. Not only did we hang out together, but we also held each other accountable, making sure we stayed on top of our schoolwork and out of trouble. We continued to care for each other after graduation, making sure that each momma's baby boy reached his full potential in life. Upon receiving my diagnosis, I met with these brothers via conference call to inform them of the news. At the end of our hour-long call, they each offered their support to Renee and the family, and prayed for a successful treatment. They remain a reliable partner to Renee, offering unwavering support and love.

When I first arrived at the hospital, Renee and I called my chapter president, Joe Rembert. He immediately galvanized our network of past chapter presidents to offer support for Renee and the family. Within one hour of notice, Brother John Reaves arrived at the hospital to sit with Renee and me for the afternoon. He offered invaluable advice on getting me transferred to Atrium's main hospital in Charlotte. We really appreciate John's offer of love and support at that much-needed time. Later that evening, I felt great anxiety awaiting any kind of news on the tests performed that afternoon. I was immediately comforted by a call from Nate, our chapter's chaplain, who offered an encouraging word and prayer. Since that day, I consistently hear from Joe and other chapter brothers, checking in on me and offering any kind of needed assistance. Most notably, the Saturday before I went to the hospital for the stem cell transplant, the chapter arranged a drive-by visit at my house. A great number of brothers came and wished us well for a successful procedure; the fellowship culminated with a dynamic prayer and reflection. This event definitely gave us the strength and will to start this procedure confidently.

"Nurse Angel"

Nurse Angel (I am using this moniker because I cannot remember her name) is a phlebotomist at the Atrium main hospital's Levine Cancer Unit. The evening of my first chemotherapy treatment, the unit's nursing staff was to draw blood and place an IV in my arm. For some reason, they had great trouble finding a vein in my arm to place the necessary tubes. Of course, this caused tremendous anxiety for me and Renee, for we were looking for this process to get started immediately. After numerous unsuccessful pokes, the nurse called down to the phlebotomy unit to summon a staff member to find a workable vein using a light source. Nurse Angel came up to the room and began her work. She is a small, older woman from India. During her search, she must have noticed my nervousness and anxiety. When she finally drew the blood and placed the IV in my arm, she began her ministry of comfort. She asked if I was a believer in God and testified that she had been in the hospital for seventy-five days, unable to move. She relied on her relationship with God to get her through her trial and encouraged me to lean on Him to get through my trial. I did not expect that ministry at that time, nor did I expect it to come from her. But I am truly grateful for God comforting and encouraging me through His vessel, Nurse Angel.

My Church Family

One evening a few years ago, Rylee and Rowan were playing with balloons in the family room. Suddenly, two of the balloons slipped from Rowan's hands and got caught up in the ceiling fan. Rylee immediately came to me and asked me to get their items down so they could continue playing. Normally, I would go right into Daddy mode and clean up the mess for them, especially this task of untangling the strings from the fan. However, in this instance, my thoughts reverted back to a Father's Day tribute I heard a few weeks earlier in church. In her tribute, Nichelle reflected on how her father always encouraged her to figure things out on her own instead of immediately running to him to solve her problems. However petty or major the issue she faced, he expected her to put the effort in problem solving before seeking his or her mother's help. She shared that this practice prepared her tremendously for the real world, for it developed her independence, resilience and self-reliance.

Perhaps Nichelle's story stuck with me because I truly admired her parents, so I channeled this practice in addressing my children's ordeal with the balloons. It was quite fascinating observing a seven- and five-year-old solving the problem on their own and untangling the balloons from the ceiling fan. They actually figured it out.

This story is an example of the productive relationships I have established with my church family. From my interaction with the men and women within the membership, I learned how to be a more productive Christian, a responsible family man, and a more confident community leader. I can testify that I would not be here at this point were it not for my church family. I am thankful for those words of encouragement when I felt like giving up. I am thankful for that special word that was ministered to me when I needed direction. I am thankful for that intercessory prayer for me when I felt down and out, and I am thankful for the opportunity to, in turn, minister to others who need encouragement.

I am truly blessed to have a caring and supportive church family. Their get-well cards, calls, and visits come in such a timely manner and provided a pick-me-up when I was down. Most notably, I found a strong partner in Mrs. Omega Hightower. Since I joined the church, I was impressed with Mrs. Hightower's caring spirit in providing information on health and wellness ministry to our church. However, I became more appreciative to become partners with her during this process. During the same time as my recovery, her husband Ernie was hospitalized with problems with his thigh. Still, she found time to send cards and call to check on me. In turn, I frequently call her to offer any assistance I could give as she cares for Mr. Ernie in the hospital. Mrs. Hightower could have easily and understandably left everything else alone and focus 100 percent on caring for Mr. Ernie. But she found time to care for me and others, even as she went through her ordeal. From this partnership, I learned that I should never use my limitations as an excuse to not be of ministry to others in need.

While I appreciate the support through the aforementioned partners, my mind continues to be led to those who were alone during their times of waiting and anxiety. Before this time, I never thought how much of a mental toll cancer takes on someone; nonetheless, a strong support system is crucial for assistance during this time. My cancer experience compelled me to reconsider my ministry track within the United Methodist Church. While I know I would enjoy leading a local congregation, I feel a greater opportunity ministering through chaplaincy, particularly to those dealing with initial cancer diagnosis. It is my hope that the Clinical Pastoral Education program assist me as I further explore the opportunity of providing clinical pastoral care to those who tremendously need support and love.

Calling

Growing up as a preacher's kid, I observed my father relying on many partners to assist in his ministry. After all, a man who pastored five churches for sixteen years had to lean on numerous assistants to serve his members. Whenever he traveled to preach at revivals, he always had one or more of his members ride with him. This person would assist with the driving and also participate actively during service, whether it be through song or testimony. The majority of his assistants would go on to answer the call to ministry.

When I began my calling experience, the conference ministry coordinators immediately stressed the importance of having mentors and partners throughout the process. I was immediately assigned to a mentorship group, consisting of ten candidates and two mentors, which met monthly to discern and share our calling and prepare for the initial committee on ministry interview. Upon completion of the interview and being accepted as a candidate, I was assigned to another mentorship group to further discuss my education process.

I learned that this partnership and mentorship structure continues throughout the ministry process. Local pastors have mentors, deacons have mentors, elders have mentors. Even bishops have mentors. Nurturing through small groups has been an effective method of discipleship for Methodists since the church's founding by John Wesley. I thank God for placing me in this structure, where I can grow, learn, and share with others as I matriculate through my ministry process.

Using Your Partners

Anyone who is a fan of professional wrestling is aware of the term "hot tag." The hot tag occurs during a tag-team match, where the member of one team is getting beaten badly by his opponent and is in desperate need of relief from his partner. The other team, of course, is doing all they can to keep the beaten opponent in the ring by any means. There are times where the beaten wrestler comes really close to making the tag, only to be deterred at the last second by the other guys. These instances are done to tease the fans and keep them excited about the eventual tag. Finally, the opponent makes the hot tag to his partner; to the crowd's excitement, his fresh opponent comes in and dominates the other team with energized and powerful moves. In most cases, the hot tag eventually leads to victory for the fan favorite.

There will be times in your life when you will face great battles, trials, and tests. No matter how hard you try to find relief or get out of your situations, it will seem your opponents are keeping you in the ring with new problems that wear you down to the point of desperation. I encourage you to remember at this point that you have a reliable tag-team partner ready to fight your battles. All you have to do is make the hot tag. Matthew 11:28 says it best: "Come to me, all who are weary and heavy-laden, and I will give you rest." Again, God wants to be your partner for any battle you face. He is ready and willing to fight with you until you achieve the ultimate victory. Just come to Him, reach out your hand, and tag Him in. He will do all the rest.

Everyone will attest that the key to a successful relationship and partnership is communication. Whatever situation arises, you must not keep your feelings bottled up inside; rather, you should let your partner know what you are feeling so you can work it out together.

I love to refer to this chart; it reminds me of the importance of consistent communication to God and to others. Whether you are experiencing joys or pains in your life, you have a partner readily available to share.

1. In our joy, we are to praise Him and thank Him for what He has done for us. He is worthy of all our praise; in no way should we get too full of ourselves to where we do not give Him thanks. As we recognize God as the source of our joy, we have no choice to thank Him for His blessing. Deuteronomy 10:21 says, "Praise him—he is your God, and you have seen with your own eyes the great and astounding things that he has done for you." 1 Chronicles 16:34 says further, "Oh give thanks to the Lord, for he is good. For his lovingkindness is everlasting."

2. And we are called to tell others of His goodness through our testimony. Our story of God's goodness and mercy can be a blessing for others; it can uplift and inspire others to follow Christ and receive His goodness. As the songwriter says, "Said I wasn't going to tell nobody, but I couldn't keep it to myself, what the Lord has done for me."

3. In our pain, we should cry out to God, tell Him of our troubles. The book of Psalms contains some of the most beautiful and emotional songs and prayers in the Bible. Whether it's of praise, wisdom, thanksgiving,

or lament, in each text, we see honest and candid expression of emotion to God. And this is how we should pray, particularly during our times of despair. Cast your cares upon Him; be honest about what you're going through. You are His child, and He will always be there to comfort, love, and guide you as you go through. Have a little talk with Jesus, tell Him all about your trouble, and He will answer by and by.

4. And we should tell others of our troubles. Despite the alarming statistics that place African Americans at higher risk of heart disease, stroke, cancer, diabetes, and other maladies, we do not see the doctor as frequently as we should. Whether it's due to the lack of affordable healthcare, lack of trust, or simply fear, we simply do not go to the doctor.

   According to Our World Data, in 2017, an estimated 264 million people in the world experienced depression. Per the Health and Human Services Office of Minority Health, African Americans are 20 percent more likely to experience serious mental health problems than the general population. Moreover, African American youth who are exposed to violence are at a greater risk for PTSD by over 25 percent. In addition to having trouble recognizing symptoms or red flags, the office attributes this rate to our general reluctance to discuss mental health issues and seek treatment because of the shame and stigma associated with such conditions in our community.

I encourage anyone who is going through a trial alone, whether it be a medical trial or other, to begin developing a relationship with God, for He is the most reliable partner you need to survive through any situation.

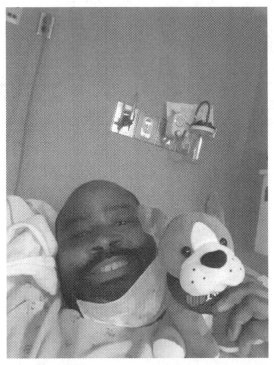

"Quentin with Tom"

Beware of the Destructive Winds

"Come," he said. Then Peter got down out of the boat, walked on the water and came toward Jesus. But when he saw the wind, he was afraid and, beginning to sink, cried out, "Lord, save me!" (Matthew 14:29–30)

The story of Jesus's miracle of walking on water is referenced in three of the four Gospels: Matthew, Mark, and John. In Matthew's version, we get a deeper perspective of the disciples' ordeal that night. After the gathering on the mountain where Jesus miraculously fed the multitude, He sent His disciples out on a ship to sail to the other side of the Sea of Galilee, while he stayed to pray alone. The disciples were out there all night, without Jesus, struggling to steady their vessel against the strong winds and waves. During the night of peril, they saw Jesus walking towards them on the sea. They were afraid and began to doubt, and as Jesus assured them to not be afraid, Peter says, "Lord, if it is you, allow me to join you on the water." Jesus then calls him with the simple word, "Come."

COVID

The COVID crisis caused many individuals to have an experience like Peter at some point in their lives. Whether it be dealing with serious illness, grieving the loss of a loved one, recovering from job loss, or adjusting to a new life of virtual gatherings, social distancing, or mask wearing, many people were faced with consequential tests of faith. During this time, some may have felt alone and lost, with no sense of guidance or direction. They may not have felt the presence of Jesus in their lives, either because they felt He deserted them in their time of need, or because they placed other priorities ahead of Him, or because they chose to shut Him out completely. Whatever the reason, COVID placed many men and women out at sea, damaged by the winds and with on the verge of destruction.

Thankfully, Jesus came to many individuals who were out at sea during this COVID crises. He not only removed their fear, but He also called them to embark on a special journey. Maybe that call was to create and build a new virtual ministry to serve and empower those strongly affected by the virus. Maybe that call was to start a new business that meets a critical need in their community. Maybe that call was to take a stand, or kneel, against police brutality—even if it means getting blackballed by their peers and losing their successful career. Maybe it was to amplify their voices and actions in protest against racism, sexism, and social injustice through the simple yet powerful phrases "Black Lives Matter" or "Me Too." Or their call may have simply been to receive Christ as their Savior and dedicate their lives to serve Him and others in love. Whatever that call may be, it is such a wonderful feeling that God has not forgotten us. He will be there to walk with us as we fulfill this new purpose. Even in the midst of this COVID mess, He remembers us and shows His love for us in so many ways.

Cancer

Peter answered Jesus's call and began to walk towards Him. All of a sudden, Peter's eyes turned to the wind, and he began to sink. As we answer Jesus's call and embark on our journey of faith, we must likewise beware of the winds and waves that can lead to failure. As rewarding as this Christian life is, as rewarding as a life of purpose is, we all can come to a consensus that life in this world is not easy. Noted poet and statesman Oliver Wendell Holmes Sr. observed, "To reach the port of heaven, we must sail sometimes with the wind and sometimes against it—but we must sail, and not drift, nor lie at anchor." How we navigate through these winds, how we deal with these trials, how we react to our setbacks determines our fate—whether we sink, drift backwards, or push forward toward the ultimate goal.

When I learned about my cancer diagnosis, I knew God was calling me to a new journey in life. Not only did I have to do what I can to fight this disease into remission, but I also needed to use this battle to grow into a more effective Christian and disciple of God's Word. As I began to trust the process and gain strength from my beloved partners, I became more confident in knowing I would come out of this trial stronger and wiser.

Through cancer, God called me out to the water. Not only did He give me the strength to complete the treatment process, but He also called me to step out in faith and more fully examine the initial calling into ministry that I answered in 2019. Like Peter, however, I found myself taking my eyes off Him many times in this journey. As my eyes turned away from Him, I felt myself sinking into a desperate state. I did not feel like going to another doctor's appointment. I did not feel like going through another chemotherapy session. I did not want to get up and get the kids ready for school. I did not want to log in for another workday at LSEG. The treatment took a lot of energy from me. I just felt like staying in bed and wasting the day away. Thankfully, I had no desire to give up, but I was close to it at times.

During this storm, winds of many kinds were pounding on me to the point lethargy. Thank God for providing me with the strength and encouragement to push on through. Whether it was through Renee and the kids, that timely phone call or get-well card, that intercessory prayer from a loved one, or a story of encouragement or inspiration, He provided enough strength to focus back on Jesus and continue this faith journey.

If God has called you out on a journey, if you are out on the water like Peter, I encourage you to beware of the following winds of destruction: doubt, distraction, division, deception, and defeat. These destructive winds have the power to take your focus away from His calling. Thankfully, God is stronger than any power or force, and with His love and guidance, you can overcome them. You will overcome them.

Doubt

First, beware of the wind of doubt.

"Will this treatment plan work for me? The doctors assure me it has a very positive success rate for remission, but what if I am one of the unlucky ones who reject the chemo?"

"You are asking me to step out on faith, but I will have nothing to fall back on if I fail."

"Did you just see what they did to you and your marchers when you tried to cross the Edmund Pettis Bridge? You almost lost your life. So why do you want to continue that march and risk your life further?"

"How are we as a church going to survive this virus shutdown? We are an older congregation; we will not trust technology to maintain our giving online, worship through Facebook or Zoom, or even use our computers to participate in meetings and Bible study. We just can't do it."

James 1:6 says, "For the one who doubts is like a wave of the sea that is driven and tossed by the wind."

. The wind of doubt is a very powerful force and can easily blow you off course along your journey. If left unmanaged, doubt leads to lack of faith, which leads to fear, which in turn results in defeat.

Part of my workout program long ago was weightlifting and body toning. To provide that extra motivation before my reps, my training partner would always encourage me to simply close my eyes and visualize myself lifting the weights and completing the rep successfully. Then keep that vision in my mind as I go through the exercise. Most of the time, that mental exercise worked; but there were times when I would be halfway through the rep and then start feeling the strain and pain. Those seeds of doubt began to grow and ultimately pushed out that vision of success.

Now, my vision of success is ringing the bell. I am walking out of that transplant unit, and I ring the bell. I have seen so many men and women ring that bell, saying that the hard work of treatment is over. Either the cancer is in remission, or it's completely gone. Whenever I feel myself facing the wind of doubt, I bring the vision of ringing that bell back into focus so I can continue my journey.

So to navigate through the wind of doubt, I encourage you to visualize success and keep that focus in mind throughout your journey. This vision will include your plan to overcome any doubts and fears you may encounter. In addition, put your trust in God to direct your paths through it all, for Paul writes in 2 Timothy, God has not given us a spirit of fear, but of power and of love and of sound mind. And that same power He gave to the Old Testament prophets as they spoke God's Word to a disobeying, powerful nation, He will give to you as you resolve to do His work.

Distraction

Second, there is the wind of distraction. In this world of instant news, this microwave society, where everything is fast paced and real time, it is very easy to get distracted from what matters most. Many of you who transitioned to work remotely during this pandemic can attest to this, for so many things around the house can easily take our focus away from our work if we are not careful. That load of dishes that need to be washed, that pile of clothes that need to be folded, or that TV show or Netflix movie you have been dying to catch.

In your spiritual walk, you face so many distractions that impede your focus and progress. You may face distractions from the past that force you to fall back on that bad habit or sin that for so long strangled you. You may face distractions from the present that keep you away from exercising your spiritual discipline. You may face distractions from the future, the urge to give into that temptation that falsely promise greater fortunes if you turn away from God. Either way, you must have a solid plan to navigate through that wind of distraction.

Jesus provided the perfect blueprint for us to follow in dealing with distraction. After He fed the multitude, He sent His disciples on a journey to the other side of the Sea of Galilee, while He stayed behind to pray alone. He found that quiet place to clear His mind, focus, and spend time with His Father. And this is what we should do, especially in this time of confusion, busyness, and uncertainty. Find your secret place, that quiet space. Free your mind, and spend that time to grow spiritually with God. As you do so, you will see a steady sharpening of focus, and like Paul, you will continue to press toward the mark for the prize of the high calling.

The strongest wave of distraction I faced came one morning in June when I was released from the hospital. I logged into work early to participate in a mandatory meeting led by our department head. To my surprise, the purpose of the meeting was to announce the closure of our operations in Fort Mill. Our jobs were being transferred to offices in the Philippines and Malaysia. Subsequently, the Human Resources representative informed me that my position would end on December 17, and I would receive a severance package thereafter. Along with the cancer treatment, I now had to deal with unemployment. Great.

Faced with this distraction, I went to my quiet place in my house to spend time with God. After prayer and reflection, God led me back to Rev. Dayson's three sermons that I referenced earlier, which reminded me that God is and will always be with me during this storm, and that God will take care of this situation if I leave my prayer to Him. God instructed me to focus on the treatment plan, for it was most important to get back to health. He would handle the job situation in due time. Though I did spend some time updating my resume and

LinkedIn profile, and applied for a couple of positions, I kept my focus on doing what I needed to do to ring that bell.

Division

Divide and conquer: this has been one of the most successful strategies in war. Once the seeds of division are sowed among the enemy, and those seeds begin to weaken their defense, you will find it much easier to infiltrate and overtake their territory. Government operatives frequently use this strategy to weaken organizations that seemingly pose a threat to its power. They send in spies and moles to enter the group and exploit a controversy or two that causes the leaders to question each other. Political administrations typically find division as their best strategy to push their agenda forward. They would exploit divisions based on race, class, religion, or gender to fire up their base and support their ideologies.

Currently, division in society is amplified through both traditional and social media. The former seemingly celebrates division to boost ratings, while social media allows users to openly express views and opinions with limited regulation. While it is natural to have difference of opinions in any environment, we trend toward danger when those disagreements allow us to become disagreeable toward others. When you are disagreeable, you do not desire to compromise. You do not want to discuss ways to coexist throughout differences. When you are disagreeable, it's either my way or the highway. All in all, you are comfortable with sacrificing your group's success for your personal satisfaction.

In his sermons about division, my father frequently referred to the story of two sisters who were members of his first appointed church in South Carolina. The ladies lived next to each other, served together on the communion steward board, and were viewed as leaders in the congregation. However, he noticed underlying friction between them. He never saw the ladies talking to or interacting with each other. As they prepared the elements, they would be on opposite sides of the altar—folding the cloth covering until they met in the middle, barely acknowledging each other. One day, my father invited each sister to meet with him to discuss their strained relationship. From their discussion, he learned that their tension stemmed from an argument thirty years ago. One sister's pecan tree overlapped into the other sister's yard, and they argued over who owned the pecans that fell into the back yard. Even after the pecan tree died, the sisters continued to let the disagreement cause them to be disagreeable with each other. All in all, they wasted thirty years of a potentially fruitful sisterly bond over a petty argument.

Romans 16:17 observes, "Now I urge you, brethren, keep your eye on those who cause dissensions and hindrances contrary to the teaching which you learned, and turn away from them." You should not allow disagreements or differences of opinion to overshadow your overall purpose, whether it be your personal calling or your group's mission or vision. Never allow divisions to turn your eyes away from God. Opportunities are always there for discussion and compromise, and if you trust God and allow Him to intervene and mediate, He will take care of any situation.

Deception

We also have to deal with the waves of deception, deception that leads us to stray from our journey into a web of sin, deception that leads us to doubt God's goodness and His

43

Word, deception that leads us to reject or stop pursuing God's special calling and turn away.

Hebrews 3:12–13 says, "See to it, brothers and sisters, that none of you has a sinful, unbelieving heart that turns away from the Living God. But encourage one another daily, so that none of you may be hardened by sin's deceitfulness."

All of us, at some point in our journey, has gone through some form of testing or temptation. If you haven't, just keep living. Ever since Adam and Eve, the devil has been busy deceiving us into the world of sin. False prophets, false idols, fake promises, "the grass is greener on the other side," this little sin will not hurt anyone—this text warns us not to allow these and other forms of deceptive sin to harden our hearts and shake our belief. It encourages us to use these tests to strengthen our Christian resolve and grow spiritually, for it is said a faith that is not tested cannot be trusted.

This text further suggests an effective way to defeat deception, which is to encourage each other daily. Friends, it is especially important to be a part of and stay involved in a strong community of believers, a community that supports, nurtures, and encourages its members as they grow in spirit and love. As I look back over my life, I can testify that I would not be here at this point if were not for my church family. I am thankful for those words of encouragement when I felt like giving up. I am thankful for that special word that was ministered to me when I needed direction. I am thankful for that intercessory prayer for me when I felt down and out, and I am thankful for the opportunity to, in turn, minister to others who need encouragement.

Let us continue to love one another, through prayer, fellowship, and support. For it is vital for us to collectively fight against those trying to turn us away from our great journey.

Defeat

Finally, there is the wave of defeat. Since my diagnosis, there have been a few notable individuals who passed away from multiple myeloma, most notably, former secretary of defense Donald Rumsfeld and former secretary of state Colin Powell. The celebrity death that affected me the most was Leonard Hubbard, the former bassist for my favorite hip-hop band, the Roots. Per his daughter, the musician was first diagnosed with multiple myeloma in 2007. The cancer remained in remission until 2021, when it came back and affected him for two months until his death. The musician was sixty-two years old at the time of his death; he was first diagnosed at the age of forty-seven, younger than me. Hubbard's death reminded me of the terminal nature of this disease. Though there are treatment plans that effectively extend the life of patients, and there are numerous studies ongoing to find a cure, there is no cure for multiple myeloma.

I am now facing the destructive wave of defeat.

Peter experienced defeat when he turned his focus away from God toward the wind. And as he began to sink, he called out to Jesus, "Jesus, save me." During your journey, there will be setbacks, disappointments, and failure. But all you have to do is call on Jesus, for the scripture says he who calls upon the name of the Lord shall be saved.

Peter cried out to Jesus, and He immediately reached out His hand and caught him and led him through the storm back safely on the boat.

Faced with the inevitability of demise from my multiple myeloma diagnosis, I cry out to God, Who assures me that death is not the end. Waiting for me is victory in eternal life. I will continue to put my trust in God, love and treat everyone the way I desire to be loved and treated, and take advantage of every opportunity to serve Him and make a positive difference in this world. I do these things, and the victory is mine.

Calling

Answering God's call is the most rewarding decision you will ever make in your life. Whatever stage of life you're in, this decision changes everything in such a positive and powerful manner. While rewarding, you will still have to manage the destructive winds that will pose threats to your success. If not careful, you will lose focus and direction—and by taking your eyes off Him and the plan, you will begin to sink.

Looking back on my faith journey, I found many instances where my eyes were directed away from His plan. Sure, I lived a pretty good life and realized success personally and professionally, but by running away from His call, I could not realize my full potential. Trust me, it is not a good feeling knowing that you are not doing what God intended in His plan; you could be doing much more than you are doing to make a difference in this world, but the voice of excuses are overshadowing the voice of potential and will.

I contend that the story of my calling experience is best expressed in the words of Bob Marley in his song "Runnin' Away": "Ya runnin' and ya runnin' and ya runnin' away … But you can't run away from yourself. Why can't you find the place where you belong?" Well, I finally stopped running away in 2019 and decided to discern His call. I felt good at first about my decision, but all of a sudden, COVID, then cancer, hit and further changed my life.

These three events were filled with instances of doubt, distraction, division, deception, and defeat. But thanks to

God, I kept my focus, determined to finally fulfill His purpose. I couldn't physically fellowship and worship with my fellow believers, but He provided the technology to have online worship services and Bible studies to keep me connected with my church and continue to grow and learn His Word. The depressing news of notable deaths, along with the over seven hundred thousand COVID-related fatalities, added extra mental stress and defeat as I initially dealt with my pain, but He provided the support and encouragement from my personal, professional, and spiritual networks to strengthen my resolve. I remain in a stalled position within the United Methodist Church candidacy process, waiting to be invited to the local pastors' school and begin the seminary training, but God provided the time, tools, and words to minister through this book. I was able to arrange God's words to encourage others to survive the destructive winds and face any situation with courage and confidence.

As with Peter, God will never leave you nor forsake you. That is the good news. Whatever you are going through, whatever winds are battering your life—doubt, distraction, division, deception, or defeat—be assured that if you call on Him, and lean to his understanding, He will guide you through the storms into a steady stream of salvation.

LESSON 4

Faith over Fear

We've come this far by faith, leaning on the Lord.

Trusting in His Holy Word, He's never failed me yet.

This lesson, Faith over Fear, reinforces what I have been taught throughout my Christian journey: the absolute power of faith. My Christian mentors have continuously taught me to lean on faith to get through any situation, and I can allude to numerous Bible lessons to assure me of faith in work. Thankfully, I have three life situations to refer back to when I testify of God's grace and mercy through faith. God is working through each situation, and because of my strengthened faith, as James Cleveland states, I don't believe he's brought me this far to leave me.

COVID

March 11, 2020, was a significant date in the COVID crisis. Around 8:30 that evening, an NBA basketball game between the Utah Jazz and the Oklahoma City Thunder was cancelled because one of the players, Rudy Gobert, tested positive for the virus. Later that evening, the league commissioner announced the suspension of the remainder of the season due to the crisis. This event caused a domino effect throughout the entire sports world, where other leagues and tournaments were paused to slow the spread of the virus.

For the first time, I really feared the virus. I lived through the Ebola scare, swine and bird flu epidemics, and SARS disease without any fear of these viruses reaching my household. However, as more sports figures tested positive with serious symptoms, I began to feel that this disease could actually touch me or a member of my family. This fear escalated when I received the news that one of my close fraternity brothers died after contracting COVID. This brother, an Army veteran who resided in Fayetteville, North Carolina, travelled to rural Georgia to work on his mother's home. There, he fell ill and died, shocking his friends and loved ones.

Subsequently, my job announced the transition to work-from-home going forward, and everyone's respective school announced the start of virtual learning to keep students and teachers safe. Suddenly, COVID was here, and as the death and hospitalization numbers began to quickly rise, so did the fear.

Because nearly everyone was relegated to home life, supply of just about everything was low. We could hardly find toilet paper, paper towels, and plastic silverware. Lunch products and snacks were tremendously low. Most importantly, cleaning supplies, Lysol, hand sanitizers, wipes, and other hygienic items could not be found online or physically in stores.

One of the first set of masks Renee bought the family during the start of the pandemic included the message "Faith Over Fear." While we made sure we followed the necessary protocols of masking, social distancing, and sanitization, this mask provided extra protection and confidence wherever I traveled because it reminded me that God will take care of me and His children, even in the midst of a scary pandemic.

The first time I traveled out of town during COVID was to attend a memorial service in Charleston. A family friend and fraternity brother, who served as a bishop in the A.M.E. Church, passed away after a lengthy illness. Along with my father, he was a noted civil rights and religious leader in the Charleston area. His son asked me to arrange and attend the fraternity's Omega Ceremony for the family. After much prayer and consultation with Renee, I graciously accepted the invitation to serve; not only did it offer the opportunity to respect our family's bond and friendship, but the trip also would allow me to visit my mother and deliver groceries to her. The fear was there, but I overcame with faith.

Like many other parents, we were faced with the decision to put Rylee and Rowan back into the classroom for school. Additionally, we had to decide whether to have Deuce continue with AAU basketball, summer team practices, and personal workouts. Though the Centers for Disease Control stated that the virus posed minimal risk to children under the age of twelve, there still existed the possibility that a child can contract COVID from an adult at the school, show no symptoms, and pass the virus to his household and close relatives. After much prayer and consideration, we allowed the kids to go to school physically, for we were satisfied with the daily COVID protocols established at both Mountain Island Charter and Cannon schools. The fear was there, but we overcame with faith.

In early 2021, we were faced with the decision of whether to get vaccinated. Amid all the chatter in the news from folks for and against the vaccine, the fear of its effectiveness and rushed approval grew in our minds, causing us to question whether it would do more harm than good to our bodies.

We decided to trust the scientists and researchers, and get the vaccine. The fear was there, but we overcame with faith.

So many individuals relied on their faith in a higher power to get them through the COVID-19 pandemic. As believers, they are thankful to God for allowing them to see new day after new day, delivering them and their loved ones from serious illness and death from the disease. They thank God for sparing them from economic calamity resulting from the economic shutdown. They thank God for providing the technological and financial resources to keep their businesses, schools, and churches operating in a satisfactory manner. They continue to believe that God allowed them to be a part of His remnant as the virus lingered on, and as part of His remnant, they have the faith that He will continue to protect and provide.

As we reflect on the past two years, through COVID and its many variants; through periods of unrest, protests, and social justice; through political insecurity, division, and insurrections; and through numerous environmental and weather-related disasters, we can truly attest to the words of Albert A. Goodson in that "we've come this far by faith, leaning on the Lord. Trusting in his holy word. … he's never failed us yet." The same faith that has brought our ancestors through many disasters, turmoil, plagues, and uncertainties remains with us, even to this very day.

Cancer

After learning of my cancer diagnosis, fear and doubt dominated my initial thoughts: *How much longer do I have on this earth to spend with my family? Will I see my kids grow into responsible adults? Will I still be able to work and support the household? If I die, will I leave enough resources to take care of my family? How will the medical expenses affect our savings? How painful will the treatment be, and will it work? Is this type of cancer hereditary? What if I catch COVID during the treatment process?*

The fear was there, but I overcame it with faith. As I consulted with the medical team at Atrium, and learned of their tremendous experience and success rate in treating multiple myeloma, I grew more confident in the treatment plan they set for me. As I consulted with my uncle Dave and Sylvia, a church member who recently overcame cancer, I became more inspired and resolved to do all I could to fight the disease. As I learned of success stories from those within my network who were living normal lives with their multiple myeloma in remission, my faith in recovery grew; that faith began to overcome and replace the doubts that previously occupied my mind.

Faith over Fear

Now faith is confidence in what we hope for and assurance about what we do not see. This is what the ancients were commended for. (Hebrews 11:1–2)

Calling

Hebrews 11:1–2 provides a great perspective on faith. Faith is the substance that links us to all that God promises us as believers, the future rewards given to those who show sacrificial love for Him through profession and action. Our faith in God moves mountains, heals sicknesses, protects us from dangers, and provides all we need as we walk this life.

My favorite analogy to personify faith is electricity. I am not an engineer, nor do I work for a power company, so I do not know the whole process of generating energy and transferring it into my home. I guess it has something to do with the dams or power plants; I don't know. What I do know is that when I walk into my home and flip the switch, the light comes on. I push the power button on my remote, and the TV comes on. You cannot see the electricity, but you see the light.

As Christians, our faith is evidenced by the Bible, which illustrates countless stories and testimonies to guide our spiritual walk. From Abraham to Noah, Solomon to David, Daniel to Jonah, Esther to Naomi, Peter to Paul, John to Peter, these biblical stories provide evidence of the tremendous faith that can make the impossible possible. Subsequently, we celebrate the revelation of Christ to the nations and God's faithfulness in showing His presence to us.

Additionally, our faith grows through our personal experiences. As we see how God blessed us throughout our journey, our confidence grows in knowing that He will continually be there for us. So in essence, our faith grows as we learn and live. We are thus empowered to share our faith stories to encourage others to grow spiritually as well.

By Faith, You Take the First Step

Martin Luther King observed, "Faith is taking the first step, even when you don't see the whole staircase." As I processed my cancer diagnosis and prepared to take the first step in the treatment plan, I definitely could not see the staircase in the process. I was not confident in the end game of the plan. Though there was evidence of the tremendous rate of success the Atrium team realized since 2014, doubt continued to permeate in my mind as to whether this plan would work for me. Will I be one of the unlucky ones who rejected the chemotherapy and other treatments? Even though I could not see the end of the road, I resolved to take that first step in the process, for the evidence presented to me outweighed the alternative, which was continuing to painfully lay in bed, immobile and unable to be the husband and dad I needed to be.

By Faith, You Keep Moving

> I just can't give up now. … I've come too far from where I started from. … Nobody told me, the road would be easy. … I don't believe he brought me this far to leave me.

This testimony, which was put into song by recording artist Mary Mary, describes the faith that allows us to keep moving in our journey of faith. After taking the first step in treatment, I found that my confidence grew with each additional step toward recovery. After each chemo session and positive test result, and as my movement gradually improved, my level of faith rose, and I resolved to finish the race to recovery. That faith impelled me to get up and exercise those days when my energy levels were so low, I wanted to stay in bed all day. That faith impelled me to ingest food and water when the medicines took away my appetite. That faith impelled me to continue that next step in the journey, when my body told me it needed a break from everything.

Two weeks after my stem cell transplant, I began feeling

overwhelmed and weary from the entire treatment process. Though the post-transplant blood count numbers were looking great, my body was still feeling the nagging neuropathy pain in my feet; additionally, the continuous low energy spells were causing great frustration as I tried to get back to normal. I was still not eating or sleeping well, and thus I resolved on many days to just stay in bed and deal with the pain. The first Sunday of 2022, Rev. Dayson delivered a very powerful message that inspired me to keep moving. He told the story of Haley Carruthers, a participant in the London marathon a few years ago. She was nearing the finish line, gearing up for a personal record finish, when all of a sudden, she collapsed on the concrete. Unable to get up, she began to crawl toward the finish line. When she couldn't crawl anymore, she started to use her arms to inch her way forward. Whichever way she tried to move, she resolved to keep her focus on the finish line and inch her way closer toward that goal.

Rev. Dayson used Haley's story to encourage us to keep working, fighting, and moving in your faith journey. Even through the difficult times, particularly when we are relegated to crawling or inching along, we should press toward that goal. God will continue to be with us as we move along; He will never leave or forsake us.

I really needed to receive this message, for it provided much-needed relief and encouragement as I grew weary of the continued pain. Through faith, I realized the awesome and consistent power of God in that He will always be with me through the good and bad times. He will give me the strength to press toward the mark for the prize of the high calling.

By Faith, You Tell Your Story

> Look Where He Brought Me From … He
> Brought Me Out of Darkness … into the
> Marvelous Light … Look Where He Brought
> Me From. (Bishop G. E. Patterson, 2006)

During a follow-up appointment from my stem cell transplant, my doctor determined that I needed to receive a shot to boost my white blood cell count. He scheduled the shot immediately after a procedure to remove the tri-fusion catheter from my upper body. Needless to say, the tri-fusion procedure lasted much longer than I thought it would, and much of my skin tissue fused around the catheter. Consequently, it took a lot out of me mentally as I anticipated pain after each tug, pull, and cut. I headed back to the infusion center after the procedure; mentally drained and physically sore, and ready to go home and rest. After checking in, I was escorted me to a chair for the nurse practitioner to administer the booster shot. As she was giving the shot, she shared her story. In 2019, she was diagnosed with multiple myeloma and went through the same treatment that I am currently on. She completed her stem cell transplant in September 2019 and was excited to be back to work. Her hair grew back, and her energy level recovered in tremendous fashion. She shared the struggles she faced after the transplant—neuropathy pain, low energy, loss of appetite, and mood swings—but encouraged me to continue to fight and be strong all the way through to the end. She assured me that those post-transplant struggles would go away soon, and I will notice myself quickly getting stronger and back to normal.

Not only did her story inspire me at a time when I was feeling discouraged, but it also exemplified how faith empowers you to share your faith journey with confidence, love, and conviction. God placed her in the right position to connect with and encourage her fellow multiple myeloma patients, and she is taking advantage of her opportunity to minister through her story. I look forward to the opportunity to share my faith story to my fellow brothers and sisters struggling with multiple myeloma, for I will be sure to share it with joy and love, like the nurse practitioner did.

Verse 6 of Hebrews says, "And without faith it is impossible to please God, because anyone who comes to him must believe that he exists and that he rewards those who earnestly seek him." Faith is all we need to receive God's favor, not extraordinary works or deeds. By faith and faith alone, we are justified and cleansed, according to God. That faith gives us a new life—a relationship with God that compels us to spread His Word, witness to others, and work for compassion and justice in this world.

"A COVID Vacation, Wilmington, NC"

See the Need, Make the Difference

> In the same way, let your light shine before others, so that they may see your good works and give glory to your Father who is in heaven. (Matthew 5:16)

I dedicate this lesson to my father, Dr. Willis Timothy Goodwin. For over forty years, my father served the South Carolina Conference of the United Methodist Church, pastoring churches in Bamberg, Easley, Johns Island, Sumter, Kingstree, North Charleston, and Moncks Corner. Additionally, he served on the board of directors for numerous organizations, which granted him the opportunity to travel around the world. He was well-known civil rights leader, advocating for equal distribution of resources to black farmers in South Carolina. His ministry was one of service and inclusion, transforming his appointed church to one where "Everybody Is Somebody, and Christ Is Above All."

From 1967 to 1982, my father served an appointment in the Sea Islands, which consisted of five churches in Johns Island, Wadmalaw Island, and Younges Island. One night, early in his ministry, a member called asking him to take another sick member to the hospital. At that time, there was no hospital or urgent care facility located in any of the islands; residents were forced to travel about a half hour to Charleston to receive care. This journey is further compounded by the drawbridges, which if open can add another fifteen minutes to the trip. My father picked up the sick member and started the journey to the hospital in the city. Unfortunately, they encountered numerous delays en route to the hospital, including an extended waiting period at one of the drawbridges. Sadly, the member passed away in the car before arriving at the hospital.

This incident deeply affected my father, for if there were a health care facility conveniently located on Johns Island, this member would have been able to get treatment more conveniently. He saw the need and began to make the difference. He subsequently started the formation of an organization to provide health care to residents in Johns Island and surrounding rural areas. The group constructed Sea Island Comprehensive Health Care, which immediately made an impact on the minority and elderly communities. Further, his rural missions ministry sponsored a retired missionary doctor from Minnesota, Dr. Harold Elliot, to provide additional medical services to the community at no cost. Dr. Elliot served the islands in this missionary capacity for over thirty years, saving the lives of many men, women, and children.

COVID

As COVID began to plague our world, many men and women saw the need to make a difference and serve others by unconventional means. Seeing their doctors and nurses physically and mentally exhausted from caring for COVID patients, communities organized to salute medical staff during nightly shift changes. Seeing many men and women in need of entertainment while having to stay home for mandatory shutdowns, DJ D-Nice started a weekend-long virtual quarantine house party, in which over 150,000 viewers logged in and enjoyed the great music and fellowship. Also, Swizz Beats and Timberland started its Versuz series, which featured music stars performing their hits in a friendly competition format. Seeing the shortage of sanitation equipment in stores, many distilleries altered their production cycle to produce and distribute hand sanitizers and other equipment that assisted in keeping more individuals safe.

As summer 2020 approached, Renee had to decide whether to operate the Young Explorers camp or not. The enrichment center realized tremendous growth during its first three years of operation, but suspending the camp for 2020 would risk losing important clientele and partnerships. The health and safety of her staff and camp members were of high priority. Further, her teachers needed the summer break to recover from the strenuous and unpredictable school year.

After further study and reflection, Renee saw two important needs. First, the majority of the enrichment center's summer camp students were from families of essential workers, essential workers who desperately needed the childcare, as they had to work. Second, the summer learning loss that many students—particularly underprivileged students—normally experience was further amplified this year due to the digital gap negatively affecting the online learning environment.

Renee saw the needs and began to make the difference. She and the Young Explorers Enrichment Center staff worked diligently to create COVID protocols and safety practices in order to offer the summer camp for the 2020 year. The camp ran effectively, with zero reported COVID clusters within the camp environment.

Cancer

Three tragic events occurred during my hospital stays, tragedies that reminded me of the importance of taking advantage of every opportunity to make a difference. During my first hospital stay in June, a condominium collapsed in Miami, Florida, killing approximately 150 residents. Residents spending a normal evening in their homes were suddenly fighting for their lives, climbing through heavy rubble from the unexpected implosion.

At the beginning of my second stay in December, a huge strand of tornadoes ravaged the Midwest, killing more than a hundred and destroying property. Men and women enjoying a normal Friday evening were suddenly fighting for their lives through the destruction from this unusual December storm. Third, the morning of my second discharge, a Charlotte-Mecklenburg police officer was killed in the line of duty. While investigating an early morning tractor trailer incident on I-85, another tractor trailer crashed into her vehicle, killing her and injuring three other officers. The fallen officer was a mother of three who just came back from maternity leave a few days before the fatal accident. She was routinely investigating an accident on the interstate; suddenly, her husband, children, and family had to spend the holiday grieving the loss of their special loved one.

I mention these sad, tragic events as a reminder that no one is guaranteed a long life; death can come at an instant and take it away. Therefore, we should value each day as a gift from God and an opportunity to make a positive difference in this world.

Since my diagnosis, I made it a point to start each day asking myself, "How can I help someone else today? How can I make this world a better place?" Also, in my prayers,

I ask God to keep me aware of any opportunity He presents to uplift someone. Thankfully, He led me to this book, for it could inspire someone else coping with a life-changing health diagnosis or struggling with discerning God's call. I encourage the reader to trust God's plan, know that you are never alone, keep your eyes on God while out in the storm, and make a positive difference, I am confident that God had led me to use these words to transform and inspire others.

The phrase "See the Need, Make the Difference" seems to limit your awareness only to the sense of sight. However, to be a fully aware and observant, you must use all five of your biological senses in the following manner:

Sight

Be aware of your surroundings, looking for any areas of need. Quite simply, if you see people in need, help them.

> Be sober minded; be watchful. Your adversary the devil prowls around like a roaring lion, seeking someone to devour. (1 Peter 5:8)

Hearing

Listen to others; this is the most important component of a conversation. Per the old adage, God gave us two ears and one mouth, so we can listen twice as much as we speak.

> Know this, my beloved brothers: let every person be quick to hear, slow to speak, slow to anger. (James 1:19)

Taste

More generally, take advantage of the opportunity to fellowship with others. The most common form of fellowship is through a meal. As you taste and enjoy a good meal, use your other senses to look for an opportunity to make a positive difference.

> Therefore encourage one another and build one another up, just as you are doing. (1 Thessalonians 5:11)

Touch

Touching is a major form of connecting with others. If done properly and respectfully, touching others lets them know you love and care for them. As you empathize with others, your heart and mind open up to determine how you can be of assistance to them.

> A new command I give you: Love one another. As I have loved you, so you must love one another. (John 13:34)

Smell

In today's pandemic, there is no better way to make a difference than to maintain a sanitary environment. By wearing a mask, cleaning your surrounding areas, and practicing great hygiene, you are protecting others from serious illness.

> And God said, Let us make man in our image, after our likeness: and let them have dominion over the fish of the sea, and over the fowl of the air, and over the cattle, and over all the earth, and over every creeping thing that creepeth upon the earth. (Genesis 1:26)

A good friend concludes his voice mail greeting with, "Today is the first day of the rest of your live. Make it count." This message continuously resonates with me, for again each day you experience on this earth is a new opportunity to do good and make a positive difference. I encourage you to use your total power and all your might to look for ways to help your others. You have the power to make a difference; do not waste that power.

Calling

The most rewarding and enlightening experience in my life was travelling with my father to the Dominican Republic for Agricultural Missions' board meeting. Not only did I enjoy spending time with him, but I also got the chance to witness and appreciate my father's "See the Need, Make a Difference" ministry in action. I was amazed at how easily he connected with the native Dominicans, despite the language barrier. During a tour of one of the poorer villages for Haitian immigrants, he arranged an impromptu collection to help one of the families. His charisma and personality connected tremendously with every Dominican he encountered during our stay; he connected so well the citizens appropriately adorned him with the nickname "El Presidente." I left the Dominican

Republic with much more appreciation, understanding, and respect for my father's ministry. Honestly, this was the first time I understood his work. Everywhere he served, he made a difference. From building new churches, starting ministries for the communities, to mentoring aspiring ministers within the congregation, he left every appointment he served 100 percent better than when he first arrived.

If I possessed a tenth of my father's charisma and leadership, I would have a successful ministerial experience. After our time in the Dominican Republic, I resolved to live and serve under the mantra "See the Need, Make the Difference."

During the Advent season, my mother always shared the following story to exemplify our opportunities to serve others:

Once upon a time, when Jesus was still in this world, there was a Tanzanian woman who wanted to make a big impression in her village. After hearing him speak as no person has ever spoken, she met Jesus in a town and asked him, "Lord, when will you come to visit us? I see you visiting other people, but you haven't come to our home yet."

Jesus replied, "Dear woman, just wait three days, and I promise to pay you a visit then."

When the woman heard this, she was delighted and immediately went home to prepare for Lord Jesus's arrival. She cleaned her house very well and decorated inside and outside with many ornaments. She hung colorful African cloths everywhere. She and her servants prepared special food and drink, especially the local beer. They slaughtered the bull they had been fattening. Having prepared everything to the best of her ability, the woman put on her finest African dress. Then she sat down and waited for the Lord's arrival with joyful expectation.

Early that third morning, a bent old man with sores on his legs appeared at her house. Upset at this intrusion, she told the man sharply, "What have you come here for? I'm waiting for an important visitor, and I don't want you messing up my house. Go away immediately."

Without saying a word, the bent old man left.

Some time later, a very old lady appeared, dressed in rags and supporting herself with a stick.

Exasperated and angry, the woman said to herself, *Why are all these things happening to me?* She rebuffed the old woman and told her, "Get out of here."

The old lady did as she was told.

Then, at midday, a badly crippled Tanzanian boy appeared. He raised a cloud of dust as he dragged along his twisted legs.

She was very annoyed when she saw him and said, "What is this wretch doing here?" She told the boy, "Get away from here as soon as possible, and don't come back again."

The boy immediately went away.

Then for the rest of the day, the woman waited patiently for the Lord Jesus, but he never came.

The next day, she met Jesus in town and said, "Lord, why didn't You come to our home yesterday? I waited and waited for You. Why didn't You keep your promise?"

The Lord replied, "My child, I came to visit you three times, but you did not receive me. When you refused to welcome the bent old man, the very old lady dressed in rags, and the badly crippled boy who came to your home, you refused to welcome me."

Like the woman, we sometimes get so caught up in our own preparation that we miss out on opportunities to serve and love others.

"Dedicated to my father Rev. Dr. Willis T. Goodwin"

GOING THROUGH IT TO GET TO IT

The morning of February 23, 2022, Renee and I rode quietly to the Atrium Levine Cancer Institute in downtown Charlotte. We both were cautiously optimistic, for we both knew the importance of this follow-up appointment. This appointment would assess the bone marrow biopsy I took three weeks earlier, which would show how well the stem cell transplant from December treated the multiple myeloma.

As I continued the check-in process, I noticed Renee's energy increasing, for she was anticipating great news. For me, I was preparing for any kind of news from Dr. Paul; I was pretty sure of the news I would receive, but with my luck, anything could happen. For any normal appointment, I would get my blood drawn before heading upstairs to Dr. Paul's office. However, the receptionist noted that today I would be getting the blood drawn after the appointment. This news added to the stress we were already feeling about this visit. Did the transplant fail? Was there a relapse of the cancer? Do I have to now begin another lengthy treatment process?

We went upstairs and asked Dr. Paul's receptionist why the order was altered. She only said an additional blood collection was scheduled, but she assured me that she did not see any bone marrow results from the collection schedule. The nurse called us back and weighed me on the scale nearby. As we proceeded back to the examination room, I overheard Dr. Paul calling my name. As we turned the corner, I saw the doctor reviewing my records with the nursing team; he had a pleasant smile on his face. We exchanged pleasantries as we passed by the nurses' desk, then in the examination room, a nurse took my vitals and made us comfortable while we waited for Dr. Paul.

Dr. Paul entered the room and, after exchanging further pleasantries, pulled up my biopsy report on his computer. Each biopsy shows the percentage of cancerous blood cells within the bone marrow. The biopsy after the stem cell transplant shows the Minimum Residual Disease (MRD), the small amount of cancer cells remaining after the treatment. Dr. Paul presented the results as follows:

June 25 (Date of Diagnosis): 15%
December 1 (Pretransplant): 1.5%
February 24 (Posttransplant): 0.0%

0 percent of cancer cells remained in my body, meaning that I was officially in remission. Moreover, because the MRD percentage was 0—in other words, MRD negative—the cancer was in deep remission. With maintenance treatment, there is a greater chance that the cancer would stay in remission much longer than normal. The stem cell transplant worked. The three rounds of chemo treatment worked. The two-week early-morning radiation treatment worked. Finally, success. This was the news we had been waiting for.

As Dr. Paul discussed the path forward with the maintenance treatment plan, I continued to think of the number 0 and the major accomplishment we achieved with the MRD negative biopsy reading. Moreover, I thought of the struggles I overcame to get to this moment, especially experiencing the stem cell transplant. I had to go through it to get to it.

The treatment plan that the oncology team prescribed for

me consisted of three phases: 1) several rounds of chemotherapy, 2) stem cell transplant, and 3) maintenance management. The first phase lasted around four months; I received the chemotherapy both orally and by stomach injection.

The first visit to the Atrium Cancer Center in Gastonia was memorable because I had tremendous trouble moving around the center. I was in extreme pain, to the point where two or three nurses had to help Renee transport me from the waiting room to the doctor's office.

As I felt myself getting stronger with each chemo session, I became more confident in the game plan for treatment. After around four months of progress, the doctors felt I was strong enough to proceed with the stem cell transplant. I was ready to move on.

The beginning of the transplant process entailed two procedures: the pretransplant biopsy and the implant of a tri-fusion port to take blood in a more efficient manner. Though the physician's assistant performing the procedure did an excellent job keeping me comfortable, I could not help but feel every bit of the biopsy. It was a very uncomfortable and bloody experience. The placement of the tri-fusion port was a little more comfortable, but the extra care I had to take was very inconvenient. First, I could not get the port wet in any way, so I had to cover it when I showered. Also, I had to watch how I positioned myself while sleeping, so I did not break any of the port lines. Lo and behold, if one of the kids decided to hop into our bed in the middle of the night, I prayed that they didn't kick or swing the port lines open. Most of all, I had to keep the port lines as clean as possible to ensure the blood could be drawn smoothly.

I was scheduled to get my stem cells drawn and collected the Tuesday before Thanksgiving. This was an eight- to ten-hour process, where my blood was transported through an apheresis apparatus that separates the stem cells before returning into my body. The cells are then harvested safely in the hospital and then placed back into my body a couple of weeks later.

The prep work for the collection proved to be very crucial, for any missteps on my part would severely delay or impair the process. I needed to take extra precautions to ensure that I was healthy enough to undergo the transplant; this included minimalizing any exposure to COVID. For five days leading up to collection time, I had to inject three sets of medicine into my stomach to boost the stem cells in my blood. This had to be done at the exact time each morning, so I had to be sure I did not sleep through the alarm, like I frequently do. Through the blood draws, chemo injections, and other procedures, my body was stuck by needles more times than I could imagine. However, this was the first time I had to inject the needle by myself; this definitely added to my anxiety, but somehow, I got it done each morning.

The day of the apheresis procedure, Renee dropped me off at Atrium at 6:00 a.m. I was wide awake, mainly due to the last self-injected shots the hour before arrival. The staff checked me into my room, and I was ready to begin. My nurse kept asking me if I had to use the bathroom, for once the machine was hooked up and the collection began, I could not stop the process for a bathroom break. Well, instead of just trying to relieve myself, I told the nurse that I was ready to get hooked up and started. Big mistake. About two hours into the collection, I had to go. However, I had no choice but to hold it in for the next six hours; talk about going through it to get to it.

In addition to the bathroom situation, I had to endure the foot pain from neuropathy. Neuropathy, the tingling sensation, numbness, and pain in one's hands or feet caused by nerve damage, is a very common side effect of chemotherapy. Most cancer patients deal with the lingering effects of neuropathy for up to a year after their chemotherapy treatment. This day, the neuropathy discomfort affected me tremendously. First, my room was extremely cold, and the thin blankets and socks the staff provided did not warm my feet. Then, my bathroom situation made it very difficult for me to stay still and keep my mind off my feet. Needless to say, those ten hours were the slowest, most mentally draining times in my life. My nurse continually reprimanded me about staying still during the process, for that help collect the millions of cells needed for the transplant. I assured her that I was trying my best to oblige, but all I could think about was getting out of that freezing room and sitting a spell in a nearby restroom.

Around 2:30 p.m., the apheresis machine finished the collection, and the nurse unhooked all the wires and patches from my body. During my follow-up appointment, I was told they had collected enough cells to continue with the transplant schedule. Valuable lesson learned, though: Always go to the bathroom before getting hooked up for a ten-hour procedure. I could have added this to the list of lessons discussed in this book, but I think it's best to keep it nestled in this chapter.

The weekend before hospital admission was very memorable, for I further realized the support of my family and friends. The kind gestures expressed through these partnerships provided the strength and will to continue through the transplant and recovery. Irvin brought my mother up to spend time with me, Renee, and the kids. We had a great time watching football (even though the Panthers lost) and sharing stories about my childhood. Most importantly, Mom was able to see me walking and moving around much better; I believe that was more therapy for her than for me. On Saturday afternoon, about thirty brothers from my fraternity chapter visited me—COVID drive-through style—and wished us well for the next two weeks. We prayed together and shared words of encouragement and support, which were received and deeply felt by the entire family. Sunday morning, Pat and Jon drove up to spend time with me and the family. Not only did they add to the level of encouragement offered throughout the weekend, but they were also able to see Mom (their second mom) for the first time in a while. We received many visits that weekend from friends and family, which probably increased the risk of COVID exposure, but we appreciated everyone's love and support. I received enough encouragement and strength to walk into the hospital Tuesday with confidence and boldness, believing everything would be all right in the end.

During the pretransplant consulting sessions, the staff explained that I would be in the hospital for approximately fourteen days, depending on how fast my white blood cell count recovered after the transplant. About two hours after being admitted, I received the chemotherapy medicine to kill all the blood cells in my bone marrow. On day three of the stay, I received the stem cells that were collected during the apheresis procedure; this was considered Day 0 of the process (more familiarly, my new birthday). From Day 0, the team monitored my blood levels until they rose to a satisfactory level. During this period, I had days where my energy level was low, to the point where I just wanted to stay in bed and do nothing. Nonetheless, the team encouraged me to move around. The floor where I stayed was very secluded; only one visitor at a time was allowed. I was required to shower every day, using special antibacterial soap to minimize infection risk. During my shower time, the nurse would refresh my bed sheets and sanitize my area. The team encouraged movement and exercise, by using the treadmill or cycle in the exercise room or by simply walking the hallway a few times, but they understood if I didn't feel like it. All in all, the staff ensured a comfortable and accommodating stay throughout the transplant and recovery process.

Everything went according to plan with my transplant and recovery at the hospital. The cells were placed back into my body without incident, and my blood count gradually ticked back up to a satisfactory level. As planned, I was released thirteen days after admittance. I sincerely thank the oncology and transplant physicians, nursing staff, housekeeping team, and nutritional group for their exceptional service during my stay. I appreciated the tremendous care they each took in keeping me as safe and comfortable as possible. Still, this hospital stay did come with some challenges for me. For the first week, an IV was connected to my tri-fusion port. I was instructed to always keep it connected, so I had to roll it along with me wherever I went. It was connected to me in the shower, it was connected to me on the treadmill, it was connected to me while asleep. This affected me both physically and emotionally. First, I had to take extra caution to not snatch the IV line from my port; this caused great discomfort and uneasiness.

Emotionally, walking with the IV took me back to the last picture my dad and I took together. While he was in the hospital, Irvin and I would accompany him on his daily walk up and down the halls. Of course, he was connected to his IV and other meds to provide some relief from his bile duct cancer. A few days before he was placed on life support, he insisted we take a picture of us together walking the hallway. So each time I walked the hall with the IV alongside, I would tearfully dwell on that picture and precious memory.

I missed my kids tremendously during that two-week period. Sure, we stayed connected through FaceTime, phone, and RoBlox, but there was nothing like being there physically with them. I had Tom lying beside my bed, but I missed being able to hug Rowan or cuddling with Rylee. Adding to this anxiety was the possibility that I would still be in the hospital on Christmas Day, missing the experience of them opening their presents. I wanted to do all within my power to build my blood counts so I could get home sooner than later.

I lost about thirty-five pounds while in the hospital. I quickly lost my appetite tying to eat the hospital food and relied on Ensure, Boost, and other protein shakes to keep my energy and nutrition levels up. I lost my taste for eggs, which was my favorite food, and all meats. My routine order with the hospital food service was sliced apples, cereal, gelatin, and toast. At times, Renee would bring pizza or Bojangles for me, but whatever I didn't nibble would stay in the refrigerator until the end of the stay. For years, I aspired to get my weight under 250 pounds, so I guess the good thing out of this process was that I achieved that goal. However, I do not recommend this weight loss plan to anyone.

I did not feel tired until about a week into the hospital stay. This was a terrible feeling. I did not feel like doing anything all day. The nurses expected me to have this feeling; they were supportive during these times and encouraged me to rest and chill. Still, I wanted to get up and move around, out of the belief that the more I moved around, the faster my blood counts would rise, and the sooner I'd be able to go home. My mind would say, *Get up*, but my body would counter, *Nobody got time for that*. The doctors prepared me for this feeling during the transplant prep, but I did not expect this lethargic feeling to be that bad.

Each evening, the nurse would collect blood from my port to check my numbers. I was prepared to watch the white blood count number to fall to 0 around day 6 of the transplant (of course, this is when my energy would be at its lowest), then gradually increase to a satisfactory level by day 14 or 15.

I recorded the test results each day, with the hope that the numbers would recover sooner than later. I wanted to be able to go home way before day 14. With this mentality, I was easily discouraged when the numbers would show a slower increase than anticipated. Even with the staff assuring me that I was progressing ahead of schedule, I allowed those numbers to keep my spirit down. This feeling, along with the appetite loss and increasing neuropathy pain, attributed to long and emotionally painful days.

The last day of my employment with the London Stock Exchange was December 17. Though I was able to work while in the hospital, I missed the physical farewell gatherings with my fellow co-workers. We did have a virtual farewell meeting a few days earlier, but I did miss physically interacting with my associates for a final time. I truly enjoyed my thirty-year career with the company. It provided tremendous growth opportunities throughout my tenure; it paid my way through graduate school, sponsored my project management and Six Sigma certifications, and fostered growth in management and leadership. Still, I will primarily remember my time at LSEG for the way I exited the company; I was notified of my termination while in the hospital, and six months later, my last day of employment was spent in the hospital.

I was discharged from the hospital on December 22, 2022, fourteen days after admission. I was truly thankful to be home for Christmas. I was able to assemble the kids' toys Christmas Eve night, while enjoying the milk and cookies the kids left for Santa; I was also able to witness their joy in sharing the wonderful gifts bought from the heart. These are the feelings I will never take for granted for the rest of my life.

I was very thankful to have this second major phase of the treatment process behind me. Even though I was home, I still had a long way to go to get back to normal. Because my immune system was still at its lowest point (the chemotherapy administered during the transplant stripped away all the vaccines I was ever administered since birth), I was instructed to stay in the house—more or less my room—for at least a month. If I had to go outside, I had to have my mask on; for not only was COVID still out there, I had to protect from shingles, flu, and other diseases I would normally be vaccinated against. Out of caution, Renee kept the kids home from school, and she worked from home the first week from winter break.

While at home, I still experienced pain, low energy, weariness, and loss of appetite. The doctors did advise me to expect these feelings for a while posttransplant, but I did not expect it to be that bad. I continued to struggle with my appetite, nibbling only bits and pieces of my food and relying on protein drinks to get my nutrition fill. The neuropathy pain in my feet got much worse at home, which caused numerous sleepless nights for me. The palliative care team at Atrium continuously worked to find the medication to ease the pain as much as possible, but nothing seemed to work. I was advised that since the neuropathy stemmed from the chemotherapy administered earlier, it would take a long time for the pain to go away. I just had to find a way to cope with the pain until it went away.

There remained two final procedures I had to undertake from the transplant process: removal of the tri-fusion port and the biopsy of the transplant bone marrow. By this time, I was extremely weary of the needles, incisions, injections, and other body invasions; however, I knew I needed to go through these last bits of pain and pressure to get to where I needed to be in the process. Boy, was there pain. Because the skin grew around and attached to the port during the month inside my body, it took a long time to cut around and remove the main part from my body. I sat through about two numbing injections and a few extra incisions before finally getting the port out from my chest. For the biopsy, I instructed the doctor that I wanted anesthesia to minimize the pain felt during the November procedure. Still, I did feel the pressure from the drilling and marrow collection. Maybe it was more in my mind, but it was a feeling I did not want to experience again.

The weariness and pain during this time did take an emotional toll on me. At times, I felt this feeling would never go away; I would be like this for the rest of my life. Sometimes, I would just lay in bed with tears flowing, praying to God to make it better. I felt the lowest the weekend in February before we received the posttransplant biopsy results. That weekend, my fraternity brothers from college got together in Charleston for a reunion and fellowship. We attended a basketball game, toured the city, and ate at a couple of restaurants. The plan was for Bacchus to fly into Charlotte from the Bahamas on Friday, and we were to drive down to Charleston Saturday morning for the festivities. While the rest of the brothers attended the game, I would spend time on Johns Island with my mom and brother.

Of course, my body had different plans. Prior to Bacchus's arrival, my energy level decreased tremendously, to the point where I could barely get out of bed. I felt much colder than normal, and the neuropathy pain in my feet increased. I really felt bad having to miss the gathering that weekend, but Bacchus was able to drive down and have a great time for the both of us.

A few days later, February 23, Renee and I listened with joy as Dr. Paul presented the results from the biopsy. The chemotherapy and stem cell transplant did so well, my body had a greater chance to keep the multiple myeloma in remission. The rest of the day, my mind replayed the song "No Pain, No Gain" by Bettye Wright.

In order to get something
You got to give something
In order to be something
You got to go through some pain.

Mrs. Wright's words were true in my situation, for I definitely went through something to get to this point of achievement: the days of immobility in my bed, the days on crutches navigating through the severe hip pain, the emotionally exhausting nights worrying about the cancer in my body, the days not being able to play with Rylee and Rowan, the nights not able to be intimate with Renee, the numerous pokes from the blood draws and chemo injections, the neuropathy pain. I definitely went through it to get to this point.

I thank God for giving me the strength and discipline to endure the pain and struggle that came along with this process. I had faith that He would place me in the hands of a capable and knowledgeable team of professionals, so I joyfully trusted the plan He set forth to take care of the multiple myeloma. The supportive network He set up throughout my life stepped up to take care of me and my family during this time. They were able to walk along with me through this journey, and their love lifted me up whenever I needed it. He gave me the strength to keep my eyes on Him throughout this journey and the wisdom and discipline to navigate through the destructive winds that could have derailed my progress. He provided numerous encouraging stories, testimonies, and examples to increase my faith during the periods of uncertainty. Finally, through it all, He allowed this situation to make the most of the remaining days of my life. I will treat each day as an opportunity to make a difference in this world.

"Bell Ringing Moment"

CONCLUSION

I write this closing truly blessed. It has been two months since I received the news of remission. I was able to fulfill my vision of ringing the bell, reaching that major milestone in my recovery process. I am currently in the maintenance therapy phase of the treatment process, with my recent follow-up appointments showing my blood levels increasing at a satisfactory rate. I still struggle with neuropathy pain in my feet, along with recovering my appetite. Still, and most importantly, I am able to get back to some sense of normalcy.

I thank God for blessing me and my family during this time. Not only has He allowed me to realize this point in the recovery process, but He also presented the lessons learned that I am sharing in this book.

"Trust God's Plan": Put all faith in God to provide and fulfill the plan He has for your life. "You Can't Do It Alone": Utilize the partners God provided for you to walk with you in your faith journey. "Beware of the Destructive Winds": Do not allow dangerous surroundings to turn your focus away from God during your journey. "Faith Over Fear": Fully rely on your faith in God to get you over any situation. "See the Need, Make the Difference": Take advantage of any opportunity to make a positive difference in your community and world.

These lessons got me and my family through COVID, encouraged me through my cancer journey, and promise to empower me as I continue my walk in faith and fulfill His purpose.

While thankful, I still have doubts about what the future holds for me and my family. When will this multiple myeloma come back? How severe will it be when it does come out of remission? How will the maintenance treatment plan affect my daily life? When will the neuropathy pain in my feet go away, and how will it affect my mobility going forward? How and when will I manage the medical bill? When will I be able to work again, and what will be my next employment opportunity? How will COVID and cancer affect my calling into ministry? Should I continue the local pastor track or venture into another area of ministry?

Numerous questions, numerous uncertainties.

So as it pertains to the future, it is best to say, "I don't know." But through God, here is what we know: God loves and cares for us, and if we trust and believe Him, He will supply all our needs. In Matthew 6, Jesus teaches, "Therefore I tell you, do not worry about your life, what you will eat or drink. … look at the birds in the air; they do not sow or reap or stow away in barns, and yet your heavenly father feeds them. … See how the flowers of the field grow. They do not labor or spin. So do not worry, saying what shall we eat or drink, or what shall we wear. But seek first his kingdom and his righteousness, and all these things will be given to you as well. Therefore do not worry about tomorrow, for tomorrow will worry about itself."

We do not know what the future holds, but we know Who holds the future. And we should walk into the future with the assurance that, because we are children of God, He will give us what we need: the right armor to fight and defeat any battle that comes to us, the right amount of food and nourishment to do His will, and the insight and revelation through His Word to minister to and love His people.

This is summed up in that great hymn: "Be not dismayed whatever betide, God will take care of you."

Printed in the United States
by Baker & Taylor Publisher Services